Why Do Men Cheat?

Featuring

Cheating—Who's Better at It, Men or Women?

Randy Wallace

authorHOUSE®

AuthorHouse™
1663 Liberty Drive
Bloomington, IN 47403
www.authorhouse.com
Phone: 1 (800) 839-8640

Published by AuthorHouse 12/23/2017

ISBN: 978-1-5462-2204-0 (sc)
ISBN: 978-1-5462-2205-7 (hc)
ISBN: 978-1-5462-2206-4 (e)

Library of Congress Control Number: 2017919413

Print information available on the last page.

Any people depicted in stock imagery provided by Thinkstock are models, and such images are being used for illustrative purposes only.
Certain stock imagery © Thinkstock.

This book is printed on acid-free paper.

Preface

$\mathcal{L}$adies, let me say this. I am not writing this book to reveal any male secrets or break any bro code. I am not trying to justify the actions of any man and what they do. I am writing this book to answer your question about why men cheat after reading my book *Relationships: the Good, the Bad, the Ugly*. It can be found on Amazon.com and Barnes and Nobles.com. Ladies, you ask me the question, "Why do men cheat, and why do they continue to cheat even when they know they have a good wife or woman at home and after they have been caught cheating?" Ladies, allow me to tell you a little about myself and why I am qualified to answer your question. I have been asked this question by both men who have cheated on their wives and wives who have cheated on their husbands. I was a player for over thirty years, and I had sex with hundreds of women, some married but mostly single. A lot of the time it was just for fun, but I did have women who paid for my special services. What I am going to do is answer your question about why men cheat and why men continue to cheat even after you have caught them. The answer is very simple, but it might not be what you want to hear. Some of you might already know the answer to that question but are not willing to accept it. Ladies, ask yourself if your man cheated on you knowing the consequences of his actions if you found out or caught him—the loss of his marriage or relationship, the loss of the love of his wife or woman, the loss of your respect and trust, the loss of his family, and the loss of his home, money, job, and reputation. Ladies, what does it say about the man you are married to or in a relationship with if he is willing to lose or give up all these things just to get a brief moment of sexual satisfaction? If you stay with him knowing that he is willing to lose all these things, what does that say about you? Ladies, I'm not judging you or downing you about your decision to stay with a man who cheats on you. Your reasons are your own. I know you say you are a good woman who will do whatever he asks you to do but you don't understand why he cheats on you. Let me say this. I know a lot of good women who have died from AIDS, suicide, or of a broken heart, and the one thing they all had in common is they all loved a cheating man. I was a player for over thirty years of my life. All my relationships were measured in hours, not months or years, and I heard all the cheating stories from men who were cheating and from their wives and women after sex during pillow talk. As a boy I witnessed the horror and the physical pain and verbal abuse that my dad infected upon my mom for thirteen years till one day she finally found the strength and courage to leave him. As a teen boy, all the men in my life and inner circle my brothers, uncles, cousins, and friends all had wives and women on the side. As a man, when my friends would marry, they would all keep their woman on the side. I never saw the love a man should have for his wife or woman, only the pain and heartache cheating cause. That led me to the conclude, why should I love and marry one woman and cheat with another woman and put her through all the pain and heartache that I saw the men in my life do to the women they said they loved? Instead I could stay single and have sex with hundreds of women and not hurt one. I have never been married, but I think marriage is a beautiful thing. It's the ultimate way for to people to show and share their love for each other, but it takes two people to make a marriage work and both have to want it to work. Ladies, toward the end of the book, I have a few suggestions that may be helpful to you when it comes time for you to choose the right man for you.

About Me

*A*s a little boy growing up, I always loved being around little girls. I loved to play with them and the way they made me feel. I loved to touch them. As I got a little older, I found out you could do more with them than just play with them. You could kiss them. I became sexually active in middle school at a young age. As a teenager, some of my friends and I would skip school and have sex parties with the teen girls who lived in my apartment complex. On the weekend nights, you could always find me up in some girl's bedroom after her mother had left for the evening. I bet there was not a teenage virgin in the whole apartment complex where I lived. When I got to high school, I lost my damn mind. I was horny all the time, and sex was always on my mind and easy to get. Having sex has always come easy for me. I have always known I had something special when it came to girls and women. I had something they liked. I didn't know what it was, but I knew I had it. The teen girls at my high school were always ready for a good time. My friend and his dad shared an apartment across the street from the high school, and that's where we took the girls for sex. At the age of nineteen I met a woman who was thirty-four years old, and she took me from a boy who would get on top of a woman and hump her to a man who could make love to a woman, body, mind, and soul. She taught me how to talk to a woman, how to hold her and caress her, and how to enter her. She taught all I needed to about a woman's body and the things I could do to stimulate a woman's body and satisfy her before we made love and make her have multiple orgasms while we were making love. And over the years, I have improved my skills to the point where there is no woman, young or old, I couldn't satisfy. After high school, I got a job at a men's clothing store on the rich side of town. There I met a guy who would change my life forever. He introduced me to the world of being a male escort or gigolo for older rich white women. For years I did this until the economy took a drive and all those rich white women's husbands lost all of their money, and they went from being rich to being middle class. There was no more play money for me, and my services were no longer affordable to them. In the late '80s I got a job working for a large uniform company. I worked there for over twenty years. I work my way up through the company from stock boy, and in the '90s I became general manager of my own store. With this job came an annual salary of $50,000 a year, a company car, a cell phone, and an expense account, and I used all these things for years to meet and have sex with as many women as I liked. This job also allowed me the freedom to come and go as I pleased, and I would have sex sometimes two or three times a day depending on what I had to do that day. I have had sex with women of all colors, race, and ages, young and old, all sizes and shapes. She could weigh ninety pounds to over three hundred pounds. It didn't matter to me. I had women who looked like supermodels and women I would only go see at night. I had women who worked good jobs and women who had a career to women who lived off government assistance. I had women who went to church every Sunday and screamed out the Lord's name in church and screamed out my name Saturday night in the bedroom. I have had sex with mothers and daughters, sometime at the same time. I was an equal opportunity player. I did not discriminate due to race, religion, or physical disability, and every woman got a turn. You can read about my lifestyle in my book *Will the True Player Please Stand Up?* It can be found on Amazon.com and BarnesandNoble.com.

Chapter 1

Ladies, Let Me Share Something with You

*L*adies, you must first understand why your man is with you in the first place. Sure, he loves you, but more than that, he needs you—and not for the reason you might think. Ladies, your man needs you to get his four basic needs met:

1. money
2. lodging
3. food
4. sex

Most men—not all men—are with their wives or women because they know they will get these four basic needs taken care of. Ladies, let me break it down for you.

Money

Ladies, think about this: there is nothing in the world you can't do if you have money. Most of the time when a man and a woman get together and enter into a marriage or relationship, the woman's income is more than the man's, and sometimes it's the only income in the home. This is because the woman is more likely to have a better education than the man she is with. This means she can get a better-paying job or career. Even though it is her money, she gladly shares it with her man.

Lodging

Ladies, think about this: most of the time when a man and a woman are together and decide to take their relationship to the next level and live together, the man is going to move into her place. Even though it is her place, she gladly shares it with her man.

Food

Ladies, your man knows you have a job or career and you have the money to buy all the food you want, and he will never go hungry or do without. Even though it's your food, you gladly share your food with your man.

Sex

Ladies, you have all of that, if you know what I mean. But you gladly share it with your man.

There you have it, ladies: your man's four basic needs. One or all of these is why he needs you and is with you. He does love you; even more so, he needs you to provide his basic four needs: money, lodging, food, and sex.

Ladies, let me start by saying two things.

First, there are lots of good men out there. They are good husbands, fathers, and boyfriends, but unfortunately, these are the men you never hear about. No one talks about these men and the good things they do for their wives and families. These are the men who love, respect, work hard every day, and care for their women and families. But we are not talking about them. We are talking about the cheaters.

Second, ladies, it is not your fault your husband or man cheats on you. His cheating has nothing to do with you. I will explain that to you later. Now this is the question I have been asked over a thousand times, and a thousand times I have given you the same answer. Why do men cheat?

Men cheat *because men want to*. I'm sorry to disappoint you, ladies, but that's your answer. There is no long, drawn-out answer. It's short, sweet, and to the point. Men cheat *because men want to*. It has nothing to do with you or the way your marriage or relationship is going or what you are doing or not doing in your marriage or relationship.

Now let me explain why your man will cheat on you, no matter what you look like or what you do for him. You could look like a supermodel and give your man all that good, freaky sex he likes and let him have a threesome with you and your best friend, and your man will cheat on you with your best friend when you are not around. If you have a new Mercedes-Benz and let him drive it, he will use your car to ride his other woman around and cheat on you. If you have a big house and you keep it clean and spotless and let him live in it for free, he will bring another woman into your house and cheat in your bedroom, dirtying up your bed. You can be a gourmet cook and make his favorite meals for breakfast, lunch, and dinner seven days a week, and what he doesn't eat he will take to the other woman he is cheating with and feed it to her. If you make $100,000 a year at your job and give him half the money, he will use it to cheat on you with other women.

Ladies, your men cheat on you *because men want to,* and it has nothing to do with you.

Now I'm going to ask you a question. Do you know why your husband or man continues to cheat on you? There is an easy answer to that question. It's because you *allow it*. Now before you get mad at me, ask yourself the below questions, and you will find your answers. Ladies, please be honest with your answers. You asked me why men cheat, and these are some of the reasons. There are lots more.

1. Have you ever caught your husband or man cheating on you?
2. Has your husband or man cheated on you more than one time and you are still with him?
3. When you did catch your husband or man cheating, did you accept his apology and his reason for doing it?

4. When your husband or man cheated on you, was it with someone you knew—a friend, sister, family member, neighbor, ex-wife, ex-girlfriend, coworker, your mother, or another man?
5. Did you forgive him for what he did?
6. Do your husband or man cheat on you and blame you for his cheating? Does he say things like the following? "You gained a lot of weight." "You don't look like you did when we first met." "You don't have sex with me like you used to and do all those freaky things that you used to."
7. Does your husband or man go out to the club or to his boys' house and not come home until early the next morning or not come home at all sometimes for days?
8. Does your husband or man enjoy hanging out with his boys drinking, smoking, playing video games, and going to the strip club more than he likes spending quality time with you?
9. Has your husband or man ever given you an STD (sexually transmitted disease) and you forgave him and continued to have unprotected sex with him?
10. Has your husband or man ever had a child or children outside the marriage or relationship and you forgave him?
11. Has your husband or man ever hit you or beat you and you stayed with him?
12. Has your husband or man ever called you a bitch, whore, or something worse?
13. Does your husband or man say or do mean and hateful things to you?
14. Does your husband or man tell you he loves you because he wants you to know how he feels about you? Or does he only say it to you when he is trying to apologize for something he has done wrong?
15. Do you think your husband or man is just as committed to making the marriage or relationship work as you are?
16. Does your husband or man compliment you on your looks and dress? Does he talk about how good other women look?
17. Do you know who your husband's or man's side chick or woman on the side is?
18. How many times has your husband or man broken your heart and you've forgiven him? Or have you stopped counting?

19. How many times has your husband or man quit a job, walked off a job, or just refused to work and you had to make sure all of the bills got paid? Or you don't want to talk about it?
20. Has your husband or man ever stolen anything from you, such as money, jewelry, your car, your furniture, or household appliances?
21. How many times has your husband or man walked out of your life and you let him back in? Or have you stopped counting?
22. Do you still have a sexual attraction for your husband or man?
23. If you could get a do-over, would you still choose to be married or be in a relationship with the man you are with?
24. Do you think your husband or man loves you?
25. Do you still love your husband or man?

Ladies, if you have experienced one or more of these things with your husband or man and you are still with him, then these are the reasons your husband or man cheats on you: because you *allow it.*

Guys, if you have done one or more of these things to your wife or woman and she is still with you, it doesn't mean you have game. It means that your good woman truly loves your dumb, cheating ass and you are too damn dumb to know it.

Ladies, your man continues to cheat because you allow it. He knows when you do catch him, you will be mad, you will cuss, scream, and yell, and you may even try to fight him, but your ultimate punishment to him is to withhold sex from him for a few days or two weeks. Ladies, your man knows he will get one or maybe all of these things done to him. Ask yourself if you were a man and you did one or more of the things listed and your ultimate punishment was that your wife or woman would withhold sex from you for a few days or two weeks, would you stop cheating? Ladies, your man, children, friends, and family can only do to you what you *allow* them to do to you. People will treat you the way you *allow* them to treat you. A man can only keep hurting you only if you *allow* him to keep hurting you. So there you have it, ladies. Your husband or man cheats on you *because he wants to,* but he continues to cheat on you because you *allow it.*

Just Call Her Baby

*L*adies, back in the days when I was having sex with all those women, most of time I didn't even know their names. This is because when I met a woman out on the town or at the club, we have some drinks, and afterward we went to my place to have sex. I would wake up the next morning not knowing or remembering her name or who the hell she was. I had to think of something to call her, so I would call her baby. For some reason, women love to be called baby, and it worked every time for me. Your man will use this word on you when you have caught him cheating. Ladies, when you do catch your man cheating, he knows the exact word to use on you to get out of trouble—*baby*. Baby, forgive me. Baby, I won't do it again. Baby, I'm sorry. Baby, I love you. Baby, please don't leave. Baby, please take me back. Baby, it won't happen again. Baby, give me another chance. Baby, it's all over with her. Baby, I will make it up to you. Baby, she didn't mean anything to me. Baby, it was only one time. Baby, I promise I won't see her again. Baby, you can trust me. Baby, I am telling you the truth. Baby, I am not lying to you. Baby, I am honest about what I am telling you. Baby, please believe me. Baby, I will change. Baby, I made a big mistake. Baby, I apologize. Baby, let's stay together for the kids. Baby, I don't know what I would do if you leave.

Ladies, does this word have an effect on you? When he is saying it, does it make you feel better about him cheating on you? After he says it, you calm down and forgive him till the next time he cheats on you. Your man knows after he is caught cheating, he can use his special magic word (*baby*) to get out of it. Ladies, here is some advice from me. The next time you catch your man cheating, put some cotton in your ears when you are talking to him so you won't hear this word and forget what you are mad about. Ladies, when you do catch your man with his other woman, don't fight her because she may not know that he is married or in a relationship. Beat his ass because he does know. Ladies, it takes two people to make a marriage or relationship work, and the only way a marriage or relationship can work is if both people want it to.

We Need to Teach Our Young Boys about Their Feelings

*L*et me say this. I am not trying to justify or condone the actions of any man. What I am trying to do is point out some of the reason men do the things they do. Ladies, as little girls you are given dolls, teddy bears, and other things you played with to show love and affection. You take care of them. You nurture them, express feelings for them, and share your emotions for them. As you grow up, you apply these same feelings when you become a young woman and mother when you are raising your family. We give little boys toy guns, action figures, and video games, some of which contain violence. We say things to little boys like, "Be tough" or "Be a man." We teach them not to show their feeling when they get hurt or when someone has hurt them. We must let our little boys know it is all right to cry when they feel hurt and pain and teach them there is nothing to be ashamed about when they show their feelings. Now he is a grown man and doesn't know how to share, show emotions, or express his feelings. He has never had to be caring or to nurture anything, so he doesn't know how. Now every child needs two parents in the home, but unfortunately, that not always the case. Unfortunately in some homes, the man in the home is not the best role model for the young boy. But we need to teach our boys about their feelings at a young age and let them know it is all right to share, nurture, express feelings, show emotion, and talk about hurt and pain. We need to teach them that it is all right to cry and show emotions when you are hurting or in pain. We need to teach them it is all right to care and express the way they feel. If we teach our young boys about their feelings when they are young boys then maybe when they become men, they will know how to express them with their wives or women, and just maybe we will have better marriages and relationships. The key to a good marriage or relationship is love, communication, understanding, caring, and sharing.

Ladies, Do You Think You Deserve Better?

*L*adies, look at that list above and ask yourself, "Don't I deserve better? Don't I deserve to be loved? Don't I deserve to be happy? Don't I deserve to live my life stress free and drama free? Don't I deserve to be in a marriage or relationship that is loving and prosperous—one built on caring and sharing and trust? Don't I deserve to have a man in my life who loves only me, and who is trustworthy, respectable, compassionate, understanding, and thoughtful and has a job and will pay the bills or at least help?"

Yes, you do, ladies. You deserve all of those things and much more. Like I said at the start of the book, there are good men out there who will give you or be all of those things to you and much more. You deserve all of those things, but you will never find them if you continue to stay in that marriage or relationship you are in with the man you are no longer happy with. You may be asking yourself, "Where can I find a good man? Where are all the good men?" Ladies, unfortunately, I don't have that answer. If I did I would sell you maps to them and make millions. But what I do have for you is some advice, and here it is: remember where you found that man, and don't go back there.

Ladies, Love Yourself More Than You Love Your Man

*L*adies, you tell me your man has given you an STD (sexually transmitted disease) and you stay with him because you say you love him, and if that's the way you feel, okay. But let me ask you this—how can you continue to love a man and have him in your life if he doesn't even care about his own life? Ladies, if your husband or man doesn't care enough about his own life to use a condom or some form of protection when he is cheating on you, what makes you think he cares about your life? Ladies, you say your man has given you a STD and blames you for it for whatever reasons. You accept his apology and *allow* him to continue to have unprotected sex with you. Ladies, ask yourself, do you love that man that much that you would *allow* him to play Russian roulette with your life? Ladies, let me say this: if your man cheats on you, he should take full responsibility for the consequences of his action. If you *allow* him to continue to cheat on you, then you need to take full responsibility for the consequence of your actions. Ladies, HIV, AIDS, and much more is out there. It just hasn't made it to your home yet.

I Want a Churchgoing Man, a God-Fearing Man

*L*adies, I hear you say this all the time. Let me share something with you: the jails and penitentiaries are filled with God-fearing men and men who go to church every Sunday. The church is filled with wife beaters, sex offenders, child molesters, murderers, rapists, killers, drug users, alcoholics, cheaters, and thieves. They go to church every Sunday. Ladies, just because a man attends church does not make him a good man. Just because he has done time or doesn't attend church regularly does not make him a bad man. What is in his heart determines the kind of man he is. Ladies, men do the things they do not because they don't fear God but because they don't fear man. Ladies, every man in his right mind fears God, but not every man who fears God is in his right mind or has God in his heart. Ladies, remember when you are praying to ask God to send you a God-fearing man and a churchgoing man, he is not the only one who hears your prayers. The devil hears your prayers, and he is in the blessing business too. Ladies, not every man who comes into your life is God sent. Ladies, let me tell you something. You are asking for a churchgoing man, and every man I know would gladly give up a couple of Sundays watching football and go to church with you if that's all he has to do to have sex with you. So ladies, think about what you are asking God for and what you want in a man, and ask yourself this: Have I showed God I'm worthy of this man from God? Have I been the woman God needs me to be? Is my life where it needs to be to accept this man from God? Ladies, that good man is out there, but you will never find him because you keep asking God for the wrong thing. I never hear you ask God for these things when you are asking for a man:

1. A man with strong family values and morals
2. A man who will lead his family and teach them how to be the family that God says they should be
3. A man who will be a good role for his children

4. A man who will be there for his children and teach them right from wrong
5. A man who will pray with his wife and family
6. A man who will work hard to support his family
7. A man who will love and support his wife
8. A man who will show and tell his wife how much he loves her and how better his life is because she is in it
9. A man who gives God all the praise for putting this good woman in his life
10. A man who will attend church with his family because he knows a family that prays together will stay together

Ladies, I never hear you ask God for this man when you are asking for a good man. Maybe that's why God hasn't sent him to you. You are asking for the wrong man. So ladies, get out and have fun dating and stop trying to marry the first man who treats you right. Remember, the devil is in the blessing and dating business too. God helps those who help themselves. If he sees you are not putting any effort into finding the right man, why should he? God is not going to send that man to your doorstep, but he will put him in your path.

Ladies, He Has Gotten Too Relaxed and Comfortable with His Cheating

Ladies, let me tell you why your husband or man brought you that STD or a child he has who you never give birth to. This is because he has gotten too relaxed and comfortable with the woman he is cheating with. He is no longer using protection. He is no longer playing it safe with her. He believes he is the only man she is sleeping with. He believes she will never cheat on him even though she knows he has a wife or woman he is cheating on her with. Men are dumb cheaters. Men believe the women they cheat with will never cheat on them. Men believe that while they are at home with their wives or women, their side chicks are home alone. He has probably been with her for a while, and she has him thinking he is the only man in her life. Now this is not typical of all cheating relationships. Most of the women that men cheat with really love or like them and care about them. But the ones who don't are the reason why you have that STD and he has a baby that you never gave birth to. It's all because he has gotten too comfortable and relaxed with his cheating.

Does He Love Her or Me?

*L*adies, how many times have you asked yourself or your man that question after you have found out he was cheating on you? Ladies, the majority of the time when a man cheats, it's more for sexual satisfaction than feelings, but with any sexual act feelings sometimes develop, especially if the relationship has been going on for a long period of time. It might not be the same feeling that he has for you, his wife, but he does feel something for her and a responsibility to her. Ladies, I know men who have been married for twenty or thirty years and had a woman on the side more than half of that time. These men live two lives, one with their wives and one with their women. These men take on the responsibility paying the other woman's bills and raising her children as well as his. These men are taking care of two homes. Some of the men raise the outside woman's children to be adults, and a lot of these children believe this man is their biological father because he is the only man who has ever been in their lives. So ladies, after you have caught your man cheating and you ask him, "Do you love her?" and he can't give you the answer you want to hear, no, that doesn't mean he loves her more than you. This means he has feeling for her and he doesn't know how to tell you, his wife, that he has some of the same feelings for another woman that he has you. Now if there is an outside child involved, this complicated things even more. You may ask him a hundred times, "Is that child yours?" and a hundred time he will tell you no. The reason for this is he already knows he has hurt you by cheating on you, and now he has to admit to you that he fathered a child with another woman. He knows this could be the end of the marriage or the relationship. He knows that you might forgive him for cheating or you have forgiven him in the past for cheating. But now he has to own up to the fact that he has fathered a child outside of the marriage and you might leave him, so he has no choice but to lie and deny, even though he knows you will find out the truth.

Ladies, Cheating Is a Premeditated Act

Cheating is a premeditated act. Whether it's done by a man or woman, it takes planning, timing, thought, and preparation to make it work. People just don't walk out of their houses and go cheat. They plan it and wait for the right time to do it. For whatever reason, a lot of effort goes into it. If people put as much time and effort into making their marriage or relationship work as they do cheating, you would have a lot more happy marriages. Ladies, think about this. Your man knows the consequences of his actions if he gets caught, but he makes that choice to cheat anyway, knowing when he gets caught he might lose you, his good and faithful wife, his happy home, his family, his money, his job, and his reputation. But still he is willing to risk all of this for some pussy when he has pussy just as good or better at home. Now what does that say about your man?

Ladies, His Cheating Can Cost You Your Life

*L*adies, I personally knew five women who lost their lives due to the fact that their spouse was a cheater and the person they were cheating with thought the only way they could be with that person was to kill or hurt his wife. Innocent people lose their lives all the time because their spouses wanted to be with another person. There are many things to worry about if you catch your man cheating other than if he made another child with the other woman, brought you a STD or HIV or AIDS, or is cheating with a crazy woman who will end your life just to start a new life with your husband or man. Ladies, do you remember the movie *Fatal Attraction* from back in the day? You saw how that turned out. The man thought he had everything under control, but his woman was out of control. The other woman lost her life, and the wife, who was innocent, almost lost her life for no other reason than her husband was a cheater.

Now That You Have Caught Him Cheating, What Do You Do?

*L*adies, I was curious to hear your answer to that question. Now that you have caught him cheating, what do you do?

1. Get mad at him.
2. Put him out of the house.
3. Cut him off from sex for a few days or maybe two weeks.
4. Set fire to his clothes.
5. Break his PlayStation or Xbox.
6. Do damage to his car.
7. Fight the woman he has been cheating with.
8. Tell all his family and friends and try to disgrace him.
9. Put it on Facebook for the whole world to see.
10. Forgive him because he said he was sorry and would not do it again.

Ladies, I left out two answers because I rarely hear you say them: I left him or I divorced him.

I Just Have to Have Some of That Ass

Ladies, most men, not all men, say this when they see a good-looking woman, and most men, not all men, will try to get some of that new ass. It has nothing to do with you. The only way I can describe the way men feel about a new piece of ass that you might understand is like this. Let's say you are out shopping and you see a dress or a pair of shoes you like, and you know you don't need them but you want them or you just have to have them. Even though you might have something similar to them at home, you just have to have that dress or those shoes. They just look too good to pass up, and you don't see yourself leaving the store without them. Ladies, your man feels the same way about that new piece of ass that you feel about that dress and shoes. He just has to have it. He can't pass it up. He knows he doesn't need it. He knows he has something similar or better at home, but he just can't pass that new ass up. Ladies, I know we are talking about two different things and that not the answer you want to hear, but that's the best explanation and comparison I can give you. My grandpa had a saying that went like this: it may not be good for me, but it is good to me. I guess the dress and shoes are in some way like that new piece of ass. It may not be good for him, but it makes him feel good.

My Husband or Man Cheated on Me and Blamed Me for It

*L*adies, you have told me this about your husband or man who has cheated on you and blamed you for it like it's your fault. Well, let me try to explain the reason for that men cheat (like I said early in the book): because they want to. But men need someone to blame or justify their cheating when they get caught, and unfortunately it's you, his wife or his woman. He will tell you about all the things you are not doing to him and with him that you once did. He will blame you and your appearance, your weight, and the way you keep the house and look after the children for his cheating. He will say things like, "You don't show me any affection," or "You don't want to have sex me him like you used to." A man will blame everybody for his cheating—his boys, his family and friends, his coworkers, or his ex. It is everybody's fault but his that he cheated on you. Ladies, the reason your man blames you for his cheating is because he is a *coward*. He is not man enough to tell you to your face that he is not happy in the marriage or relationship and he wants out. He would rather blame you for him not being happy than tell you the truth—that he wants out of the marriage or relationship. Ladies, that's why your man blames you for his cheating. He is a *coward* and is not man enough to tell you the truth.

The Truth Is the Truth Even If It Is Not What You Want to Hear

People sometimes have a hard time accepting the fact that a marriage or relationship is over. Sometimes men and women do not want to accept the fact that it's over and it is time to move on. Sometimes people will not accept the truth about a situation if it is not the way they think it should be. People sometimes hear what that want to hear rather than believing the truth as it has been told to them. If a person no longer wants to be in a marriage or a relationship, then people need to accept that fact and move on with their lives. I know you might say you gave him all of your best years and now he wants to up and leave you. I say to you that your best years might be ahead of you, but you will never know if you stay with a person who doesn't want to be with you. Now you might say, "What about all those things I gave him? I want them back." Ask yourself, did you give him those things to make that person happy or did you give him those things because you want to feel better about yourself and what you are doing or not doing? You might say to yourself, "I did all those things for him and now he wants to leave me." Now ask yourself, did you do those things from your heart, or did you do those things to make yourself feel better? The truth is the truth. Accept it no matter how you feel and move on with your life.

Viagra, Cialis, Crack, and Get My Nails and Toes Done

*L*adies, these things have put an end to a lot of marriages and relationships, and they have made it hard for older women to find and keep an older man. Let me explain.

1. Viagra and Cialis: Ladies, before the invention of these drugs, men over forty, fifty, and sixty who had problem in the bedroom or who couldn't get it up pretty much stayed at home. You know that old saying, ladies—if it can't get up, it can't get out. Ladies, you know what I mean. Some men have gone for years living with the embarrassment of knowing that they are not able to sexually satisfy their wives or women. Ladies, now that this man has these drugs, he can take a pill and a few minutes later do things sexually that he hasn't been able to do in ten, fifteen, or twenty years. Now he is fifty-five but he feels like he did when he was forty-five— and he has the hard-on like he did when he was thirty-five—so he is looking for a woman who is twenty-five. Ladies, now he is able to do something he hasn't been able to do in years—get a hard-on or get it up. Look out, women of the world. This is all because of a little blue pill. Ladies most men use the drug the way it was intended, for sex and intimacy with their, wives or women. Some men lose their damn minds and try to screw every woman they can.

2. Crack: Ladies, since the invention of this drug, the pimping profession no longer exists, and the pimps now have to work an eight-hour job just to make ends meet. Back in the day when a woman would sell her body, she would take the money to her pimp. Today when a woman sells her body, she takes the money to the crack dealer. Back in the day every woman who was tricking had a set price for what she would do sexually. and that was that was pretty much the same for every woman no matter you wanted for your money. Now that you have so many women on crack, the

prices have changed. These women will do a lot for a little money. They will do something strange for a little change. They will love him long time. He can get all of his freaky fantasies satisfied for less money. Ladies, I bet you are saying those men who are messing with those young women on crack could get HIV or AIDS. Ladies, let me hip you to something. There are lots of older women, mothers, and grandmothers out there who don't use crack and have HIV and AIDS. Men know these women can give them HIV and AIDS too. They are just willing to take that chance.

3. Get my nails and toes done: Now ladies, this is the going price for sex for some women, young and old, and this price is very affordable to men. I remember back in the day if a man wanted to have sex with a woman, he had to come to her with something—pay the mortgage or rent, car note, utility bills, or buy some groceries. Now all he has to do is buy me some crack or get my nails and toes done. Ladies, I am in no way degrading or belittling any woman, but the name of the book is why men cheat, and these are some of the answers. Men cheat because it is so affordable. Now all of these things make it hard for women and older women to find a man over fifty who wants to get married or be in a relationship. Ladies, now you know another reason why men cheat. It is affordable.

Blame It on the Economy

Ladies, due to the economy and people's economic situation, everybody is trying to get more for their dollar. That in itself has hurt the dating game. People just don't have the money to do the things they used to or go to the places they went to. Ladies, because of this some older men (not all older men) are seeking the company of younger women because it might cost less to date her. Some young women (not all young women) are looking for a quick payday from older men, and he is looking for a good time without having to spend a lot of money. This is not to say that if a man wanted to date an older woman he would have to spend a lot of money. That is not the case. These two people normally know where to find each other, and when they get together, they know what they want.

Why Men in Their Fifties and Sixties Are Not Looking for Marriage or a Relationship

*L*adies, this is another question that you have asked me, and the answer I'm about to give you may not be what you want to hear or one you will understand, but it is the truth. By the time most men (not all men) reach this age, they have gone through or are going through one of more of the following: raised own children and some cases their grandchildren, divorce or lost a wife that he was with for years, or is dealing with health or financial problems. Now he finds himself single again and trying to date. He may or may not be looking for marriage or a long-term relationship, but he is seeking companionship with a good woman. Now he meets you a nice lady in her fifties or sixties, and he is thinking maybe he can start a new life with you, but there is one problem he sees: your children and grandchildren.

Your Children or Grandchildren May Be Keeping You from Happiness

Grown Children Living at Home

Ladies this is how most men (not all men) see this. He has raised his family and has dealt with his own problems that came with that. Now he does not want to deal with yours. Some mothers and grandmothers (not all) still have grown children living at home for whatever the reason. Most men (not all men) believe when children reach an age where they can take care of themselves, they need to be on their own, especially if the child is a boy and does not have any health, mental, or physical problems. A man feels he should be on a job and not on his mother's couch. Now he will often make exception if the child is a girl. The reason for this is in most cases, not all cases, the grown children can be disrespectful toward him. I have seen this and been told this by stepfathers. Ladies, some of you (not all of you) allow you children to be disrespectful toward your man, and when he leaves you, then you wonder why. This is why he didn't allow his own children to disrespect him, and he is damn sure not going allow your grown children to disrespect him, not even for you.

Your Bad-Ass Grandchildren

Ladies, how many times has someone said that about your grandchildren? Ask yourself how many times have you said that about your own grandchildren. Now most of them (not all of them) are out of control, don't mind, and are very disrespectful to you and other people. They talk back and do as they please, and you expect a man to come into your life and accept this behavior. Many of you might be saying, "He might have the same problem with his own grandchildren." Yes, he might. If he won't deal with this behavior at his own home then what makes you think he will deal with this at your home?

Can We Reschedule? I Have to Babysit?

Ladies, I am in my late fifties and have never been married. Now I am trying to find that special lady to spend the rest and best years of my life with. I am finding that to be impossible, not because the older women aren't out there but because they are too busy babysitting or watching the grandchildren (not all but some). I have stopped counting the number of times that grandmothers and I had to reschedule a date or cancel our plans so she could babysit the grandchildren. It was not because an emergency came up or a situation came up that needed their parents' attention. No, but it was because the grandmother is the babysitter, and no man is going to change that. Now ladies, I don't know how many times I have heard you say you have raised your children and now it's time to live your life. Grandmother, if you live your life, who will be there to babysit the grandchildren? Grandmother, if you are living your life, then how can your children live their lives? They can't go out and have fun because they don't have a babysitter. Grandmother, how many times have you told a man you had to reschedule after you have made plans to go out on a date? Grandmother, your daughter didn't come get the grandchildren when she said she would. Now you have to cancel your plans. Grandmother, your son or daughter had something to come up and needed you to watch the grandchildren. You have to take the grandchildren to their appointment because for whatever reason, their mother or father was not able. How many times have you changed your plans to have a good time or go out on a date just to accommodate your children's plans for fun or to go out on a date? Grandmother, men know you love your children and grandchildren and you will do anything to help them. Men don't have a problem with that and understand that. They just don't want to take your children's babysitter away. Now ladies, those are two reasons I hear a lot coming from older men. Some (not all men) older men don't want to date older women because they do not want to be disrespected and damn sure don't want to be at home with you on the weekend babysitting the grandchildren. Ladies, your children are glad that you are not dating. If you did meet a nice man and start dating him, then they would not have a babysitter to keep the grandchildren on the weekend.

Older Men Only Want Younger Women

*L*adies, that's not true! Not all older men like dating or are only looking for younger women to date or be in relationships with. Yes, there are a lot of older men who do enjoy the company of younger women, but the majority of older men still prefer a classy, intelligent, sophisticated, and mature older woman. Now some older men (not all older men) believe when it comes to sex, older women are not as willing to try new things as some younger women. Now ladies, keep this in mind. Here is a man who hasn't been able to have sex for months or years. Now he can take a little blue pill and stay hard for hours. He might not last for hours, but he will stay hard for hours. He can finally do all those freaky things he has heard about or seen on video but was not able to do or get his wife or woman to do. Now ladies, I bet some of you are saying, "If he were doing the right thing by me and keeping his ass at home, he could get some good, freaky sex at home." Yes, you are right, but let me try to explain something about men. I am not trying to justify or make any excuses for the action of any man. Back in my day as a player, you did not only have to be good with women. You had to understand women and understand what they are going though at a certain age. I did, and that's why I was so successful with women, young and older. I did research and learned all I could about a woman's body, young and older. The majority of men don't know or don't understand when a woman reaches a certain age, her body starts to change, and this change will affect her mood, personality, sex drive, and health. Most men (not all men) think when a woman reaches a certain age, she just gives up on sex altogether. He doesn't know or understand sex can become painful or uncomfortable for her because of these changes and her body and health problems. All he knows or understands is he is not getting sex from his wife or woman, and he does not understand why. Most men will not ask why or try to find out why his wife or woman feels this way. His answer to that problem is to go out and get sex with another woman, not knowing the woman he is with just might be going through same things his wife or woman is going through, but he doesn't notice it because he is not with her long enough to see it. Now on the other hand, women are much more understanding when it comes to the change in a man's body, like ED or erectile dysfunction or he can't get hard. Most women will not run out and find a new man. She will show him love and understanding and support him. She will care for him and stay with him because she knows a good marriage or relationship is not built just on sex alone.

The Cost of Dating a Younger Woman

Now like I said, some young women (not all young women) are just looking to keep up their appearance, party, and have a good time. Not all young women are looking for a sugar daddy or a man to take care of them. Another thing, ladies, that you may or may not have noticed is today a lot of younger women are only dating young women and not older men. Now let me break down the cost of dating these women.

1. Get her nails and toes done—forty dollars.
2. Get her a chicken a two piece chicken dinner—eight dollars.
3. Get her some weed, beer, or liquor—ten dollars.
4. Get him a little blue bill—ten dollars.
5. The cost of a single condom—two dollars.

Now the evening is set. She has what she needs and she is going to give him what he wants, all for under seventy dollars, and a good time will be had by all. He has stayed within his budget.

A Date with an Older Woman

*N*ow an older man knows that a date with and older woman will cost him more and he will probably get less are nothing out of it. Now the cost to date (some older women not all older women) seen thought the eyes of an older man.

1. Play or concert tickets for two—$140.
2. Dinner and after—$50.
3. Gas—$20.

Total for one date night—$210. Now I am not saying all dates with an older woman will cost this much, but this is about average. What does he get after spending all that money? Nothing, not even a kiss, but if he is lucky he might get a church hug from you. Ladies, not all men are looking to have sex with you on the first date, but ask yourself if you were a man and you just spent a week's pay on a woman for a few hours of her time, wouldn't you want to get something out of it?

Ladies, I am not saying all young women are cheap and easy to date, and I am not saying all older women take a week's pay to date. What I am saying is times are hard, money is hard to come by, and men and women are just trying to get the most for their money, and that includes when it comes to dating. Don't blame the older man for looking for a cheaper date. Blame the economy.

Older Women, Get You a Younger Man and Be Happy

*N*ow let me talk to the older women. As you know, if you are a woman over the age of fifty, it is very hard to find a man to date who's your age. If you are a woman over the age of sixty, it is almost impossible to find a man to date. Now I hear you say all the time, "These younger guys are always trying to hit on me or talk to me." I say go for it. Be like the older men. Get you a younger man and have some fun with him when you need him. Now I know some of you are saying, "No way, I am not dating a younger man." I say you are missing out on all the good benefits, and here's why. Ladies, I know a lot of you have a BOB (battery-operated boyfriend or vibrator) in your nightstand or closet, and you use him when you need to release some tension or you just want to have an orgasm. That's okay, but wouldn't you rather have a man to massage your body, caress your breast, rub your booty, and do all those other freaky things you like done that BOB can't do to you? Ladies, you know what I mean. A young man will do all of these things and last longer. If you can't find an older man to do those things, get you a younger man who will and you will get much better results. Some older women say older men are just like Monday—they come too quick and sleep too long. Now ladies, if you do decide to get a younger man then there are rules to follow, just like men do when they date younger women. Here are the rules.

1. Keep it strictly business. Keep your feelings out of it.
2. Agree on a price, and let him know what you expect for your money.
3. You always select the meeting place. Never go to his place or let him come to yours.
4. Only take your drivers' license and enough money to do what you need to do.
5. Never pick him up or let him bring a friend.
6. Never let him drive your car, and make sure you always tell someone you trust where you are going.

7. Always make him take a shower before sex and demand he wear a condom.
8. Don't keep going to the same hotel or motel. Change it up.
9. Do not tell him anything about you or your family.
10. Be safe and use caution.

Ladies, those are the rules men follow when dating young women. Now some of these rules will change as you get more relaxed and feel more comfortable being around your young man. Remember, you are not his mother. He is only there to fulfill a need. With that said, go out and enjoy that younger man.

Cheating Doesn't Always End a Marriage or Relationship

*I*n some cases, a marriage or relationship can survive adultery and cheating. I personally know friend and family that stayed together twenty, thirty, forty, and fifty years after their spouse was catch cheating. But the marriage was never the same. I never understood how a person could stay in a marriage after his or her spouse broke the vows that he or she made before God, family, and friends to forsake all others and love only you. I have never been married, but I think marriage is a beautiful thing and the ultimate way for two people to share and show their love for each other. Why a person would choose to do something that might cost him or her that love I don't understand. I guess you have to be a cheater to know the answer to that question.

Cheaters, ask yourself these questions.

1. Is my marriage worth saving?
2. Am I willing to lose what we both worked so hard to build?
3. Will cheating make my marriage or relationship better?
4. Would I want my spouse to cheat on me?
5. Is the person am cheating with better than the person I am married to?
6. Other than good freaky sex, what else do the person am cheating with and I have in common?
7. If I put as much time in making my marriage work as I do cheating, would my marriage get better?
8. What do I have to gain from cheating? Will it make my marriage or life better?
9. Is cheating my only option to fix the problem I'm having in my marriage?
10. I know if I get caught cheating it will hurt my spouse, so why do I continue to cheat?

Were You His Other Woman or His Side Piece before You Became His Wife?

*N*ow ladies, there are two sides to cheating. We talked about the man. Now it's time for you to take responsibility for your actions. Some of you might get mad, but I don't care. A man can't cheat by himself. It takes two people, a man and a woman. Now ladies, let me ask you some questions.

1. Were you the woman on the side before you became his wife?
2. Were you friends with or did you know that man's wife before you cheated or took her husband?
3. How long did you pursue that man before you finally got him to cheat with you? Weeks, months, years?
4. When you start sleeping with him, did you know he was married?
5. Did you care if he was married?
6. If you had known that he was in the married in the beginning, would it have made a difference in your choice to sleep with him?
7. Did you care or not care that if his wife found out he was cheating with you he might lose his wife and family?
8. Did you deliberately get pregnant thinking he would leave his wife for you?
9. Have you ever called, harassed, or stalked that man's wife?
10. When you did get that man, did he turn around and cheat on you like he cheated on his wife?
11. Did you think he would be faithful to you knowing he was not faithful to his wife?
12. Is your life better now knowing that you took that woman's husband and broke up her home and family?
13. How do you feel now that you have that man?
14. Do you believe in that old saying what go around comes around and one day some woman might cheat with your husband?
15. Are you proud of yourself knowing that you are sleeping with another woman's husband?

16. Do you think his wife deserves what he is doing to her while cheating with you?
17. Do you think he loves you more than he loves his wife?
18. Do you think he loves his wife more than he loves you?
19. Did he get an STD from you that he gave his wife?
20. Now that you have him, are you as happy as you thought you would be?

Now ladies, I have to be honest with you. These are the questions that came from wives whose husbands have cheated on them. They told me they just wanted to know how the other woman felt about cheating with their husband. And they also wanted me to deliver this message to you: Google the song "I'll Be the Other Woman," and men, you Google, "It's a Thin Line between Love and Hate" and "If Loving you is Wrong I don't want to be Right" and listen to the words.

Ladies, He Needs You to Cheat with and You Allow It

*L*adies, we have addressed why men cheat. Now it's time to talk about the women they cheat with. Some women see cheating with a married man as a way of getting what she wants from him, like money and the bills paid without putting in the time, hard work, or effort like the wife has put in. Some women think if they can be a better woman to him than his wife is then he just might leave his wife for her. Women who knowingly have sex with or date a man who is in a marriage or relationship is wrong, just like the man who is cheating on is wife. But they don't care. It is all about what they want and need. The other woman, the side piece, the jump off, the chick on the side, THOT (that hoe out there)—these are women with no morals and values and who have low self-esteem and are not concerned about the consequences of their actions. Ladies, these are the words that the wives and the women of the men you are cheating with use to describe you. They are not my words. These are the words many wives and women use to describe the women who are cheating with their husband or man. There are many more, but you get what they are trying to say. Ladies, another reason why men cheat is because they have someone to cheat with. He knows that his side woman will accept the fact that she will always be the woman on the side and that is good by her as long as he can pay some bills and help her out from time to time. She is willing to give him what he wants when he needs it. The majority of the women men cheat with accept this position and gladly stay with him for years. This woman accepts his lies and everything he tells her about the wife or woman he is with, even though she knows in her heart it is not true. She knows he still has some love for this woman because he is still with her and won't leave her even though he says he is unhappy. He stays with her, and all the while he says mean, hateful, and bad things about her. She will continue to cheat with him, and all the while, she is convincing herself she is doing the right thing for him. In her eyes, she is not a bad woman. She is just a woman who fell in love or has strong feelings for a married man. This is the how she justifies her cheating actions. She is just giving him what he is not getting at home. This is the lie he has told, and this is the lie she chooses to believe. But in the back of her mind, she knows she is wrong for this. She often thinks about if one day when she finds her a husband or man, he will have another woman on the side just like her. She knows that this is something she will have to deal with in the future, but for now her only concern is keeping this married man happy by doing whatever it takes to get money and keep the bills paid. Ladies, this is another reason why men cheat, because the woman on the outside allows him to cheat with her. So to all the wives and the women out there who have a husband or man who is cheating, you don't only have to deal with a cheating man, but you also have to deal with the woman who allows him to cheat with her. Cheating will never stop unless both people involved want it to. And men will never stop cheating as long as there are women out there who are willing and allow him to cheat with them.

Ladies, He Feels the Pain

*L*adies, let's say you caught your husband or man cheating and you put him out and the marriage or relationship is over. Even though he is gone, you still miss him and you hurt because he is not there. But you see him out and about, and he looks like nothing has happened. It's like he has gone on with his life. You ask yourself, "How can he do this? How can he just act like nothing has happened? How can he just go on with his life and I am going through so much hurt and pain?" Ladies, the answer is he is hurting as much or more than you are. Remember, earlier we talked about how young boys are taught not to show pain, feelings, or emotions. This is what he is doing. He will experience the hurt, pain, and emotions of losing a good woman like you, but he will never show it. Even though he seems happy on the outside, he is experiencing the same hurt and pain you are because he knows he hurt you and he lost a good woman. He might not never tell you or show it, but he is hurting. He is in pain just like you are, but he will hide it just like he has been taught to do.

My Cheating Story

*Y*es, I have a story to tell about cheating. I lost the only woman I ever loved over thirty years ago because I was a cheater before I became a player, and ladies, there is a difference. I will explain it to you later. I was in my twenties when I met this girl named Sharon. When I first saw her, I knew I had to have her in my life. She was a very beautiful young lady, and she had everything I was looking for in a woman: pretty face, small waist, big breasts, and a big, round booty. Remember now, I was in my twenties. She was new to town and lived with her grandmother. Her grandmother was an old-school churchgoing woman, and she was not letting any guys who lived in the apartments she lived in get close to her granddaughter. I used to live there and now I hung out in the apartments with my friends. I would see Sharon and her grandmother sitting out on the front porch and going to and coming home from church. I knew she would be mine. One day as I was on my way to the apartments, I saw Sharon and her grandmother walking from the grocery store with a few sacks of groceries in their hands. I pulled over and asked them if they wanted a ride.

Grandmother looked at me and asked, "Do I know you?"

I said, "No ma'am. I used to live in the same apartment you live in and am on my way there to hang out with some friends and I will give you a ride if you like."

She said no at first, but it started to rain hard. Then they get into the car. The grandmother and I started to talk. She asked me if I had a job. "Yes ma'am," I answered. She asked if this was my nice car I was driving. "Yes, ma'am," I answered. She asked if I had my own place. "Yes ma'am," I answered. She asked me if I went to church. "Yes ma'am," I answered.

She asked, "Are you married?"

"No, ma'am," I answered.

I had a feeling that grandmother felt a little bit better about me now. We made it to the apartment, and I helped them take the groceries to their apartment. When we were inside, Sharon asked me if I wanted to buy a raffle ticket from her for her church. They were raffling off a TV. I asked how much were the tickets.

She said, "One dollar."

I said, "Give me ten."

She said, "The raffle is in two weeks, and you are welcome to come to it."

I said, "Okay, I will come and pick up you and your grandmother for church if that's all right with your grandmother."

The day of the raffle came, and we went to church. I didn't win the TV, but after church I took Sharon and her grandmother out for dinner after we made it home. Sharon and I sat on the front porch and talked for a while. After we were done talking as I was about to leave, I asked her for her number, and she gave it to me.

I asked, "Is this okay with your grandmother?"

She laughed and said, "Yes, she likes you."

We talked on the phone and then started to date. I didn't know at the time she was a virgin, and she didn't know I was about to put an end to that. We dated a few months. Then she moved in with me, and my life was great. I had a woman I loved, and we were very happy. A year or so went by, and then I went back to my old ways—cheating and staying out all night or just not coming home at all. We started to argue all the time, and I would say mean and hurtful things to her and she would cry. One day we had a bad argument, and I told her to get out. As soon as I said it, I knew I didn't want her to leave, but my male pride would not let me tell her that. Sharon went to the back room and called her dad in Houston. She told him she wanted to come home and she needed him to come get her. They talked for a while, and then he asked to speak to me. We talked and started to argue, and I told him he didn't have to wait till next week to come and get his daughter. I would put her ass on the next plane to Houston. I call Southwest Airlines and booked her on the next plane going to Houston. I told her to pack her things. I was taking her to the airport. As she packed, I could tell she didn't want to leave, and in my heart, I knew I didn't want her to leave.

I loved this woman, and I was just going to let her walk out of my life because I was not man enough to say, "Stop, I want you to stay. I am sorry."

On the way to the airport, I would look over and see the tears coming down her face, but what she didn't know I was crying inside. When we arrived at the airport and she got out of the car, she turned and looked at me with tears in her eyes and said, "Randy, I love you."

When she said that, it was like everything I felt for her came out. I started to cry. As she turned and walked away, I felt a pain like I never felt before. This pain was deep in my soul. When she got on that plane for Huston, she took a large part of my heart with her. To make matters worse, I found out months later from her cousin that she was pregnant and lost our child because she was so stressed out over our breakup. I was devastated. I not only lost the love of my life, but I caused her to lose the life of our unborn child.

"God, what have I done? Father, please forgive me!" I asked.

Well, that was over thirty years ago, and I have never felt that way about any woman again. What I am saying is you might only get one chance at true love, guys. Please don't blow it like I did. Because I wanted to be a player, a cheater, it cost me more than I was willing to lose: the only woman that I ever loved, and her love, the security, and the comfort that come with being in a relationship with a good woman. I miss all the other things that come with being with her. I lost all of these things while trying to be in a relationship and trying to continue to live a player lifestyle. But I learn two things from all of this: 1. A man is not measured by how many women he can make love to, but he is measured by how well we can truly love one woman. 2. Remember, guys, you might find out too late like I did that she wasn't just a one-in-a-million lady but a once-in-a-lifetime woman.

After losing Sharon, I made a promise to God and to myself that I would never cause another woman that hurt and pain and put her through that hell again. I knew I was not ready for a relationship or marriage, and I let the women know it up front. That was the start of my player lifestyle, and for over thirty years I lived it and I sex with hundreds of women. I was looking for Sharon in each one of them. Every one of those women knew what kind of relationship I wanted, and it was her choice to be with me or not. That's my story, and I hope someone will learn from it. For over thirty years I have been dating and having sex with all of these women just trying to stop the pain in my heart I felt from losing Sharon.

The Difference between a Player and a Cheater

*L*ike I said, there is a difference between a player and a cheater. Here is the difference.

A cheater is a man who is in a marriage or relationship and he steps outside of that marriage or relationship to have sex with another woman. He is a liar, schemer, or pretender, and he uses these things to meet and mislead women into having sex or a relationship with him. He will say anything or do anything for her just to gain her confidence. This is the only way he knows to get a woman. He uses deception and misrepresentation to his advantage to take advantage of women.

A true player like I was back in the day was a single man—a man not in a marriage or relationship and who is free to date and have sex with as many women as he wants. A true player like I was back in the day was up front and honest with the women he was involved with. He told the women what kind of relationship they could expect from him, and he let it be their choice if they wanted to be with him or not. He knew not every woman would accept what he was offering, but he still let it be her choice to be with him or not. Even though he didn't love one woman, he cared about all the women he was with. He knew if a woman was willing to give him her body then she cared something about him. He also knew if a woman had a child or children, she would always need help financially, and he would let her know that he was always there for her. A true player like I was didn't try to control a woman, but he was not going to be controlled by any woman. A true player like I was back in the day was more than a lover. He was someone a woman could count on in her time of need. There you have it—the difference between a cheater and a true player like I was back in the day. If you want to read about my lifestyle as a pimp, true player, gigolo, and male escort, go to Amazon.com and BarnesandNoble.com.

Ladies, Get Yourself a Check for Your Years and Your Tears

*L*adies, let me ask you something. Do you have a life insurance policy on your husband or man? Ladies, don't you think you deserve something for all of those years you were with him and all of those tears you cried over him? Don't you think you deserve something for the mental, physical, and verbal abuse he put you though for years? Don't you think you deserve something for all those night you were up worrying about him if he was safe? Don't you think you deserve something for those lies he told you and all those broken promises he made and didn't keep? Ladies, if your husband loves you, he will make sure he takes care of you while he is here, and he will make sure you are taken care after he is gone. Ladies, there is nothing wrong with praying for the better, but you must also prepare for the worst. Ladies, some of you spend ten, twenty, thirty years, and more with that man, and when he dies, you get nothing but his last name, and unfortunately, some of you ladies don't even get that. The reason why I ask, ladies, is because I am damn tired of pitching in money on these damn fools' funerals all because that damn fool you call a husband or man thought his ass was going to live forever. Now his dumb ass is dead, and you have to raise money to bury his ass. You are asking people to pitch in so you can raise money to bury him. Let me say this to you. You pitch in on food, gas, weed, beer, alcohol. You shouldn't have to pitch in to help bury this damn fool because he didn't have life insurance. Ladies, get yourself a life insurance policy on your husband or man. You don't have to harm a hair on his head to collect because one day his lifestyle, health issues, and running those streets will do it all for you. He might tell you he has a life insurance policy on the job or his mother, daughter, sister, or aunt has one on him, but let his dumb ass die and you try to get what is coming to you and your children and see what will happen. She will act like he was her husband. Now you have to try and figure out how to bury him. You go to your church and ask them for money and you couldn't ever get his ass to go to church on Sunday. After that you will try to borrow money from family and friends, and they will lie and say they don't have any. Next you go to your job and get money from your 401k. Even after his dumb ass is dead and buried, he is still stressing you out from the grave because you are trying to figure how to pay the bills he left you—the mortgage, car note, and credit card debt, and all the other bills he made. Ladies, get yourself a life insurance policy with your name on it, and when that day comes and he does pass away, you can go to that insurance company and get that big check with your name on it. You bury him, pay off your bills, take care of your children, and take the rest of the money and take yourself a cruise and lay up on some exotic beach with a pretty colored drink in your hand with that little umbrella in it and get your groove back.

Women, Let Me Empower You with This

*Y*ou are in control from the first hello to the last good-bye. There will not be a first date, relationship, or marriage if you don't allow it to happen. Women, you are CEOs of corporations, you are heads of states, you can run countries, you are doctors and lawyers, and you can give birth to a child and raise it on your own. You make decisions that will affect or change the world; you make decisions that will affect or change lives, but when it comes to the decision to change or better your life and leaving that no-good man, some of you are like deer caught in headlights. You don't know what to do about that husband or man. Most of the time the decision you make is not the best one for you. God has given you something that no one else on the planet has, a superpower. It is called women's intuition. With this superpower, you have the ability to feel and know when something is not right. But when it comes to a man, you lose your superpowers. You ignore your feeling and go against your intuition. Ladies, if your husband or man is willing to lose all the things we talked about just for a few moments of sexual satisfaction then your marriage or relationship is already over and you are not willing to acknowledge it. Ladies, for whatever reason you choose stay in that bad marriage or relationship, I wish you the best.

Ladies, think about men's basic needs: money, lodging, food, and sex. Now ask yourself, do you think your husband or man is still with you because he loves you after you have caught him cheating, or is he still with you because he needs you to supply his four needs? Ladies, a lot of men don't know what a functioning relationship or marriage is because a lot of men have never been in one. My granddad had a saying that went like this: if a person doesn't know much, a person can't do much. Women, remember, this he might be a man's world, but you are in control of your life.

Communication, Understanding, Dating, Relationships, and Marriage

*L*adies, at the beginning of the book I said we would talk about some things that may help to make to a better choice when it comes to finding the right man for you. The things I have listed above are where I have seen you having the most problems. Maybe I can help you with them. Let's talk about them.

Communication and Understanding

I think these two things are very important to the success of any marriage or relationship. There are more, but I have seen these two things must be in place. They are the foundation that every marriage and relationship should be built upon. Once you have that, then you start to build up love, trust, and respect. These things must be in place before a relationship can evolve into a marriage. If you have these things in place, you stand a very good chance with having a good life with that special person. Please be honest with that person about what type of relationship you want to have with them. There are all types of relationships—friends with benefits, friends for finances, or friends to have a good time to party with. There is nothing wrong with these relationships, but make sure the person you are involved with knows what he or she can expect for you and make sure you let him or her know what you can expect from him or her.

Two Years Is Long Enough

Ladies, this is a question I get asked all the time. How long should I be in a relationship with a man before we take it to the next level or marriage? If the dating process went well and you are now at the next level of relationship, you want to know how long we stay at this level before we go to the next step of marriage. I say two years, and here is why. I am going to break it down in six-month periods.

The first six months I call best-behavior period. The first six months is when two people enter into a relationship. They are on their best behavior. They are trying to impress each other. They say and do all the right things. They leave the room when they have to fart, they close the doors when they have to pee, and they are on their best behavior trying to impress each other, so they do everything right.

The second six months is the boo period. Now that everything is worked out with you and your boo, you can always be seen together. You are inseparable, and all your friends and family hear from you is, "Me and my boo." They are very happy for you that you have found someone to make you happy. But they are damn tired of hearing about you and your damn boo.

The third six months is planning a life together. Now if you have reached this stage, congratulations. You've been together a year, and you are probably living together and one or both are you are thinking about marriage. This is when you should start asking the person you are with about his or her plans for the future and if they include you.

The fourth six months I call making a decision. Now you have been together with this man for eighteen months, ladies. You feel very comfortable with him—so comfortable that you can go into the restroom while your man is shaving his face, and you sit on the toilet and take a piss in front of him. Then yes, you two are ready for marriage. Now it is time to make a decision about your future and your married life together. There should not be any doubt in his mind if he wants to spend the rest of his life you with. He has had two years to make up his mind, and if he is still undecided, then it is time for you to move on. Don't waste years with a person that likes what you do for him but doesn't want to marry and commit himself to you.

There you have it, ladies. I say two years is the length I think you should wait. A lot of you will disagree and that's okay, but ask yourself how long you were in your relationship before you took it to the next level of marriage and how that worked out for you.

Dating

Dating is a way to gather information about a person. It is a way for two people to come together and exchange information about each other. You can see if you want to take it to the next level in a relationship. There is no sex in dating, and both people are free to date anyone they want. Remember, dating is just away to gather information about a person. You should take as long as you can to try to find out as much about the person you are about let enter into your life and your child's or children's lives. Ladies, in my years of being a true player, I have found out this is where most of you make you mistake. You confuse dating a man and having sex with that man to mean you are in a relationship with that man. No! Ladies, men do not see it that way. If you have sex with him without a commitment from him, that's a win for him. If you have sex with a man while doing the dating process, then you have lost your control, and he now has control. Remember, you are in control of everything. Nothing will happen unless you allow it to happen. If you don't have a commitment from a man, you are not in a relationship with that man. This is the way men see it. Like I said, there is a difference between dating and a relationship. While dating you are trying to get to know that man. In a relationship you are trying to build something with that man.

Relationship

I think relationships are a good thing to be in. It is a way for to people to come together and share that special bond. Relationships are better when two people are committed to it and each other and no one else, and both people have each other's best interests at heart. A good, strong relationship has to develop over a period of time and should not be rushed into. People sometimes think just because you like a person and you enjoy being around him and he makes you feel a certain way you and that person are in a relationship. No! The person you are with might not see it that way. He might just like having you around. Ladies, here again is where some of you make your mistake. You think having a sexual act with that man means you're in a relationship with that man. Ladies, men don't see it that way. Just because a man has sex with you does not mean he is committed to you and you two are in a relationship. Men don't see it that way. That's why is so important to establish a good line of communication and have a good understanding with the man you are with about your relationship and where it stands. Ladies, you make this mistake all the time having sex with a man before you have a commitment from him. Then when it doesn't work out, you are mad and upset. Ladies, if you have sex with a man before he commits himself to you then you are not in a relationship with him. You are just having casual sex with him.

Marriage

I have never been married, but I think it is the ultimate way for two people to show their love for each other. A good marriage takes hard work from both people, and it is formed over a period of time. The two people must be able to stand up to life's challenges. They must be able to weather life's storms and the obstacles that lay ahead when these things happen. The two people will stand together and face them head on. Marriage is an institution that should not be entered into if there is doubt or distrust. People enter marriage for other reasons, such as lust, convenience, greed, or circumstance. Remember that not all marriages are meant to be. Not all marriages will last forever. At some point your marriage will end. It may be because of death or divorce or some other reason that's out of your control. When your marriage ends, you might be left confused, devastated, and heartbroken. However, you will get over it. You can move on with your life, and you will love again. There is no shame or disgrace if your marriage ends. They end every day. The shame is staying in a marriage or a relationship that you know you need to get out of. If it doesn't work out, cut your losses and move on. Don't spend years in a marriage or relationship that you know in your heart is not going to get any better. Ladies, remember this—not all boyfriends will make good husbands, and not all husband will help you make a good marriage. There is nothing wrong with praying for your marriage or relationship to get better, but sometimes your only option is to pray and pack. A marriage shouldn't end just because a person gains weight, his or her looks change, or his or her desire for sex is not like it used to be or you are having health and financial problems. All these things fall under the category for better or worse. Remember, they were in your marriage vows. Every marriage will have its problems, but you should try harder to find a solution to your problem and not by running into the arms of someone else.

Now Let's See If We Can Help or Save a Marriage or Relationship

*N*ow everybody knows that it is very hard to introduce something new into a marriage or relationship, especially when it comes to the bedroom. Some people are just not open to change or are not willing to try new things. Let's go back to the beginning. You both vowed to love each other and forsake all others. Now that phrase *forsaking all others* does not mean turn you back on your family and friends. It means you two are the only lovers you should have. Now you have been together ten, fifteen, twenty, or more years and the marriage or relationship has gone stale or has no life. You are wondering, *What can I do to put some excitement and life back into my marriage or relationship?* Like I said earlier, introducing something new into the bedroom is very hard, but in these times, some people believe bringing a third person into the bedroom might help spice things up. Some people tell me that it worked for them, but most people say it caused more problems than it solved, and here's why; when you bring a third person into the marriage or the bedroom, it's more of a personal thing than a *we* thing. It's just like cheating, but your spouse knows about it. It's only going to benefit one person. Then after the act is done, you still have the same problem. Now ladies, I know you have been told go out and buy some sexy lingerie and prance around in front of him and that will turn him on. No! Let me tell you why. As a man that has been selling ladies' lingerie for over fifteen years and owns his own business called Randy's Luscious Lingerie, let me tell you this lingerie looks better when it's on the floor. Ladies, if your man is not turned on by the sight of you with your T-shirt and panties on or your boy shorts and a bra or some booty shorts and a tank top, there's a problem. It doesn't matter what size or age you are—every woman looks sexy in those things, and if that don't turn him, nothing will. You take that the money you just wasted on that lingerie and use it to get you nails and hair done.

I would tell the ladies who bought my lingerie, "Buy this for yourself because it makes you feel good to wear it, and if your man is smart enough to realize the benefits he might get by you wearing it, then okay."

People need to get back to what worked for them. Do you remember that old song, the something it took to get your baby hooked? It's going to take the same thing to keep her. Ladies, do you remember when your man would do something simple like make you laugh and how much joy that brought you? Guys, do you remember how a homecooked meal not only filled your belly but would relax you after a long, hard day at work? It was the small and simple things you did that made your man or woman happy back in the day, and they still work today.

Get Yourself a Goodie Bag

Every marriage or relationship should have a goodie bag in the closet or under the bed. This bag should be filled with things for both him and her to make the lovemaking experience more pleasurable, satisfying, enjoyable, and fun. Step outside of your comfort zone and be adventurous, and experiment with new ways to make your lovemaking better. Like I said, it may be difficult to introduce something new in to the bedroom with most men, and some women have a problem with it too. But when you start a new marriage or relationship, don't allow it to become average or routine.

A True Player Goodie Bag

*S*ome of my clients had special and unusual requests for me, but I didn't mind because it paid well. I was the man my special clients called to satisfy their unusual needs. I also used my goodie bag just to have fun with the women I was having sex with. All the women loved my goodie bag, also known as my little bag of tricks, and they were all crazy about BOB.

What My Goodie Bag Was Filled With

*I*nside of my goodie bag was a bottle of Jack Daniel's, a bottle of wine, a six pack of Magnum condoms, two XXX-rated movies, body lotions, flavorful oils, a tube of KY Jelly, a jar of Vaseline, a couple of power bars, an energy drink, a bottle of water, Tic Tacs, and a Marvin Gaye Greatest hits CD. And BOB. Most women call him their battery-operated boyfriend. All the women loved BOB. He was twelve inches long and three inches around with a head that wiggled from side to side and back to front. BOB glowed in the dark. BOB was big hit with all the ladies, and that made my job easier.

Lovemaking

*L*ovemaking does not start in the bedroom. It ends up there. Lovemaking starts with a, "Good morning. Have a good day. How is your day going? How was your day?" People, lovemaking starts with letting the other person know that you do care about him or her and how he or she is doing. Lovemaking is an expression of feelings though words or a sexual act. People need to know and feel that they are loved, just like you made them feel when you two first got together. Instead of trying something new in your marriage or relationship, try something old. Make love to that person using your words and showing emotion. Express the why you feel not with a sexual act but with an act of love and kindness. Do the things you two did when you first got together.

Do You Remember Back in the Day?

*D*o you remember back in the day when you and your man would slow dance to your favorite song? Do you remember back in the day when you two were dancing he would pull you closer to him and he would start to grind you and his hand would always end up on your booty? Do you remember back in the day when you would sit in your man's lap and pick the hairs out of his face and all the while his hand was trying to make it up your dress? Do you remember back in the day when your man would grease and scratch your scalp and how good that felt? Do you remember back in the day when you two would just sit and watch TV for hours? Do you remember as you two were watching TV, his hand would always end up on your breast and you liked it? Do you remember back in the day when you would put the kids to bed early so you and your man could have more time to spend together? Do you remember back in the day when you and your man would spend hours drinking, smoking, and playing spades or dominoes? Do you remember back in the day when your man would paint your toenails, and all the while he was trying to look under you dress? All of these things worked for you and your man back in the day. Why can't some of them work for you and your man today?

When where the last time you and your man or woman did these?

1. When was the last time you and your man or woman took a bubble bath together?
2. When was the last time you rubbed your man's or woman's feet?
3. When was the last time he gave you a back massage?
4. When was the last time you gave him a back massage?
5. When was the last time you and your man or woman went on a weekend getaway?
6. When was the last time you cooked his favorite meal?
7. When was the last time you cooked her favorite meal?
8. When was the last time you sang his or her favorite song to him or her?
9. When was the last time you two made passionate love, not sex?

10. When is the last time you two went to church together?
11. When was the last time you two prayed together?

These are just a few things people tell me they did when they first got with that man or woman they are with. There are lots more. My question to you is if they worked then, why can't they work now? People, remember, you don't have to introduce something new into your marriage or relationship to make it work. Why not try something old? It worked before. It just might work again. Just try it. You might still like it.

Distraction

This is another reason why marriages and relationships don't last. I know in these times, people are distracted by a lot of things. The same things that are meant to make our lives better are breaking up our marriages and relationships. Distraction will take place outside of your home, and there nothing you can do about it, but you can control the distraction in your home. Let's take a typical home—not all homes but most. When a man makes it home, the first thing he does is look for something to eat and something to drink. Then we turn on the sports channel or get out the PlayStation or get on social media, like Facebook something else. Now when a lady makes it home from work, it's a little difference. She just might want some me time alone just to sit and think, and she might have cold drink or a glass of wine and reflect on her day. Then she gets on Facebook or social media, and this is how the two of you spend your evening before bedtime. You might have the occasional sex that you put no effort into. This might not be exactly how the evening goes, but I am not too far off. There is no conversation or interaction between you two. You are now more like roommates than lovers. People, you need to find a way to work together to remove these distractions from your life. You need to try to reconnect with each other. You both have to want it to work before it can work.

Get out of That Damn Dating Routine

*P*eople, I hear you say this about your marriage or relationship. It has become a routine. It's in a rut. Here is the reason why you are doing the same things and you are expecting a different result. That's the definition of insanity—doing the same thing and expecting a different result. You have to mix things up and try new things, not only in the bedroom but in life. Go to new pleases, try new food, and try to experience new adventures and things together. For your marriage or relationship to grow, blossom, and bloom, you two must first plant that seed and nurture it and do all the things you both can do to make it grow.

Experiencing a True Player

*L*adies, I have told you what a true player I was. Now I am going to tell you why I was so successful and able to date and have sex with hundreds of women. It was not because I looked good and smelled good, had money, had a job, had my own place, had a nice car, or was a gentleman. No! That was not the reason, but all of those things did help. The reason why I was so successful—take notes, ladies, there will be a test at the end—was because I challenged women to step outside of their comfort zone. Now these are the things you would normal do on a date: movies, dinner, lunch, club, dancing, drinks, plays, bowling, concerts, or a walk in the park. This is not a date. This is a damn routine. It is just like the routine you do every morning when you get out of bed. You shower, wash your face, brush your teeth, comb your hair, and put your makeup on. This is your routine. You do these things every morning without thinking about them, and that's the way you date. You do the same damn things without even thinking about them on every date with every man because it has become a routine to you, and that is not your fault. Let me explain why. It is because the man you are dating, that's all he knows—movies, dinner, lunch, drinks, dancing, plays, concerts, bowling club, or a walk in the park. He does these things with every woman he dates because he knows that this is what you will expect, and he does not have to change or try something new with you. Ladies, you must show that man that you are not his average, routine woman. Ladies, back in the day when I was a true player, male escort, man whoa, and whoa mongo, I was all of these things and the women loved it. Why? Because I kept my appearance up. I was well groomed. I went to the beauty salon twice a month just like you do to get my nail and toes done and a facial. Ladies, I know hundreds of men, and none of them ever had their nails and toes done. I did these things because women like a good-smelling, well-groomed, soft man who has no toenails or fingernails that will hurt her, especially when she is paying good money for him. Ladies, men see you after you have had these things done and see how good it makes you feel after. Most men wonder what would it be or feel like to have it done. Ladies, how about for a first date, take

him with you? In doing this you have just sent him the message that you are no average or routine woman and you will not be treated like one. Do not expect an average or routine date from any man. If he does not want to step his game up, then you leave his average and routine ass alone. If you start off like this, he will only give you what he has been giving every woman he dates—average and routine.

Why I Was So Successful

*W*hen I first met a lady, I would ask her to write down the five things she liked doing. Then I would take that list and come up with five things she had never done before. Then I would ask her to list her five favorite foods, and I would come up with five new foods for her to try. I would ask her to write down her five favorite places she liked to go, and then I would take her to five places she had never been. Ladies, I did this with every woman I was with because I knew not all women are the same. Not everything works for every woman. I would take their list and come up with a different plan for each individual woman. I would save the best for last. After dating for a while, I would ask her to list her five favorite ways she liked to make love to and the five things she liked done. I would take that list and come up with five ways that no man had ever made love to her, and I would do things to her that she had never had done to her. Ladies, that's how I was so successful with women. I took them out of their routine. Like I said, it is not your fault you don't know what a real date is like. It's because the men you have been dating didn't know. My hope is one day, ladies, you will experience what it is like to be with a true player like I was back in the day.

Your Bedroom Is Meant for Two Things Only

I will leave you with this. Your bedroom was designed for two purposes only—to sleep in and to make love in. You need to remove all other distractions from it, such as TV, laptops, computers, radio, books, video games, and cell phones. These things distract you from enjoying your bedroom and what it was designed for—making love and sleeping. Good night and enjoy.

Guys, Technology Is Putting an End to Cheating

*G*uys, let me say this. If you have a good wife or woman, stay with her and treat her right and leave all those other women alone. Technology is putting an end to cheating, and you are not smart enough to know it, but your smart wife or woman does, and she is using it to bust you and you don't even realizes it. Let me explain it to you.

GPS: Girl Personal Surveillance

*G*uys, this device is used by your wife or woman to keep track of you 24–7. With this device she knows where you are at all times and you don't even know it. It sends her a signal to let her know when you are on the move. This device can be put in your cell phone, car, or laptop, even your wallet. You don't even know it's there and you are being tracked. She knows when you leave your job, house, club, and any other place you go, and this is how it works.

Tracking a Dumb Fool

*G*uys, let's say you are at home and you tell your wife or woman that you are going over to your boy's house to hang out. As soon as you leave the house, she activates the GPS device. She knows your boy lives on the south side of town but you are going north, so she calls up a girlfriend to ride with her, and now they are tracking you and you don't even know it. The only thing on your mind is all that good, freaky sex you are about to get. So you pull up at you girlfriend's house or apartment. You get out your car and go inside. You get relaxed and comfortable. You have a drink, and now you are ready to get your freak on. Now there is someone banging on the door like the police yelling for you to bring your ass outside. You get up and go look though the peephole of the door and see it's your wife or woman outside trying to get in, and she is screaming for you to bring your ass outside. Now your girlfriend comes to the door to see what is going on. You are trying to keep her from opening the door. Your wife or woman is banging on her door, and she is asking you what is going on. "Who is that woman outside, and what does she want with you?" She's asking this because you told her you were single, and now your wife or woman is at her place trying to break down the door to get to you. The next sound you hear is some glass breaking and a brick or bottle as it comes through the window. She is outside screaming for you to bring your dumb ass out, and you are inside trying to explain to your girlfriend why you didn't tell her you were married or in a relationship. Now do you do the right thing and go out and tell your wife or woman that this woman didn't know you were married or in a relationship? No! You keep your cowardly ass inside, where you think you are safe. A few minutes go by, and there is no more banging on the door. Things are quiet, and then there is a knock at the door, You peep though the peephole. It's the police, and they want to talk to somebody. You and your girlfriend step outside, and you look at your car. Your windshield is caved in, and your headlights are knocked out. Both mirrors are on the ground. The taillights are knocked out. The twenty-four-inch tires are all flat, and *dumb bitch* is keyed into your car.

The police ask you, "Do you know who did this?"

You look at them with that dumb cheater look on your face and say, "No, sir."

Now all this has happened, and you still didn't get any freaky sex from your girlfriend and you're damn sure not going to get any from your wife or woman. It's all because your dumb ass cheated, and your smart wife or woman busted your dumb ass with her GPS.

There is hope for you, cheater. Just listen to Randy.

Okay, guys, there is still a chance you can get your wife or woman back and save your marriage or relationship. If you do the things I am about to tell you every day, I promise your wife or woman will forgive you and let you come back home.

1. Stop the cheating. Be the man she needs and know you can be.
2. Beg her for her forgiveness for all the lies and broken promise you made to her.
3. Do everything you can to earn her trust, respect, and love.
4. Show and tell that good woman you have how much you love her and how much better your life is because of her.
5. Make her feel special every day. Make every day a special day for her.

Guys, I promise you if you do these things every day and continue to do them every day, that good woman will let you back into her life and heart.

Now, guys, those things will get you back in the house, but if you want those home-cooked meals and the good, freaky sex she was giving you before you messed up, then you must step your game up. Get a pen and some paper and take notice. A true player is about to tell you something. There will be a test at the end.

1. On Monday make sure she has a clean car with gas in it and lunch money for the week.

2. On Tuesday do something nice for her. Cook her favorite meal and have it ready for her when she comes home. Have a hot bubble bath and a glass of wine waiting.

3. On Wednesday after you get home from work, spend some quality time with her. Talk to her and find out what's on her mind. Sit down with her and watch her favorite movie or TV show with her. Make her feel like she is still your boo.

4. On Thursday if you have young children, make this family night. Do something with your wife and your children. If not, the two of you should just play cards and talk. It's all about being with her.

5. On Friday make this treat my baby right night date night. Take her out on the town and show her a good time. But be creative, not routine. Do something different with her like you did back in the day when you were trying to get her.

6. On Saturday help her around the house with the cleaning. Take the children where they need to go so she can have some time to go shopping. Run some errands or get her hair, nails, and toes done. On Saturday night, you take that good woman and make love to her like you did when you first met her. You make wild jungle monkey love to her. You turn her upside down and around and around. You spank her booty. You lick it up and lick it down. You make her scream when she is not afraid. You make her body tremble and shake when she not even cold. You knock her wig off her head. You sweat her perm out. You loosen up her weave. You make her moan and groan. You make her cry when she is not sad. You knock the bottom out of it, and then you stand up in it and look down into her eyes and ask her, "Who's your daddy?"

7. On Sunday you take your family to church. Remember, a family that prays together will stay together.

Remember, guys, you were once this man. You can be this man again, but you must want to be him. You know that old saying that one man's trash can be another man's treasure. What you may be taking for granted another man will get and worship.

Well that is the end of the book. Ladies, I hope I helped you to understand why we men do the things we do. I hope I helped you to find the answer and make the right choice about your marriage or relationship. Just remember, not all marriages or relationships are meant to be. Remember, ladies, your husband or man cheats because he wants to, but he continues to cheat on you because you allow him to.

Look for These Books

*I*f you'd like to gain more insight about relationships, read my books *Relationships: The Good, the Bad, the Ugly* and *Will the True Player Please Stand Up* or visit BarnesandNoble.Com and Amazon.com or visit my website randywallacebooks.com. Be blessed.

I'd like to thank God, my mother, and my family.

Thank you God, my Father.

First I'd like to thank God and give him all the praise for bringing me though the madness that was my life. I know if it had not been for his grace, love, mercy, and forgiveness, I may have been killed or died from HIV or AIDS living the lifestyle I was living.

Thank you, Mom.

I would like to give a special thanks to my mother, whom I love very much. Thank you, Mother, for your love and support over the years. I know I kept you on your knees praying to God to watch over me and keep me safe. I know if it had not been for you being a woman of God, something bad would have happened to me years ago. I bet when you were on your knees praying to God and when your prayers reached him, he would look down on you and say, "Oh no, not Randy again." Mom, I know I was not the best son you had, but you were the best mother any boy could want. Thank you, Mom, and I love you more then you will ever know

Thanks to Bishop Kevin Willis and Pastor Linda Willis

Thank you and your ministry. I know I didn't attend church like I should, but you never judged me and I was always welcome in your home and church.

A special thanks to my little sister

A special thanks to Linda Willis. You were not only my pastor; you were my life coach, counselor, spiritual advisor, and psychologist, and I needed all of that. The best thing about it she didn't charge me anything. Thank you, Pastor Linda Willis, and I love you.

Thank you, family and friends

You would always tell me, "Boy, you need to get
some Jesus in your life." I know, and I did.

Thanks to that old school church sister

Thank you for those years you lived under me in my apartment
and saw me running different women up and down my stairs and
you never said a word. All you would do was stand there with
your arms folded and shake your head from side to side and say,
"Son, I am praying for you." Thank you all, and be blessed.

Cheating Who's Better at it, Men or Women?

Contact me by email at

rwrelationship@yahoo.com

Facebook
Randy Wallace of Dallas, Texas

Preface

I have written this book as a follow-up to the *Will the True Player Please Stand Up?* I've been asked by men, "Why do women cheat, and how can I tell if my wife or woman is cheating on me?" I tell them the majority of women are not cheaters. It is not in their nature. In my own experience, I have had sex with married women and women who were in a relationship. This is what I learned the majority of the time when women cheat, it is because of three reasons: anger, revenge, or a broken heart. There are many more reason, but these three were the ones I heard the most. Men asked me how could I tell if my wife or woman was cheating on them. I tell them "You can't, and here's why. Women are very selective and creative cheaters, and the majority of the time a man will never catch his wife or woman cheating unless she wants him to." I hope this book will give men a little more insight about their wife or woman and what made her cheat. This book is by no means meant to belittle, disgrace, or put down any woman. But I do hope it will open the eyes of the men/women who are cheating so they can see the pain they are causing to their spouse. I have been asked by men and women how was I able to have sex with so many women who were married or in a relationship. Let me say this—I was not out to break up a man's home or take a man's wife. I was only there to give that woman what she was not getting at home. I never tried to replace that man. I was just the man she needed at that time. Cheating is a conscious decision that an individual makes. The action of a person husband or wife may play a big part in his or her decision. I have never been married, but I think marriage is a beautiful thing. I think it is the ultimate way two people can share their love with each other. Back in the day, all the guys in my inner circle cheated on their wives or women. I would ask them, "If you love her why do you cheat on her?" I never got an answer, only excuses.

The Three Types of Cheaters

*I*n my opinion, there are three types of cheaters. You may know more, but from my own personal experience having friends and family members who are cheaters, I have found out that there are three types of cheaters.

1. The Justifiable Cheater: This cheater can be a man or woman who cheats. He or she thinks he/she has a good reason that justifies his or her act of cheating. It can be payback or revenge for something someone has done to them. It can be for other reasons, like "I'm not getting what I need from the man or woman I am married to or in a relationship with." Or "The person I'm with has changed. He/she is not the same person he/she was when we first got together." Or "We have grown apart. We no longer do anything together." Or "We have lost interest in each other, and we never do anything together. I am bored or tired of the same old things and want to try and experiment with new things, and he/she doesn't want to."

2. The Curious Cheater: This cheater is more common in women than men, and here's why. Ladies, how many times have you heard your girlfriend, family members, or casual associates brag about how good her man sex is in the bedroom? She talks about how long and large he is and all the good, freaky tricks he can do with his tongue and all the positions he puts you in and how long he can last. She makes its sounds so good that you just have to try it for yourself. You just have to see if he is all that. Your curiosity has gotten the best of you, and you just have to try it for yourself. Ladies, we men lie a lot and brag a lot about all the women we are having sex with. The majority of us men are curious cheaters. We see a woman and think what it would be like to have sex with her all because she has a pretty face, big breasts, a small waist, and a big, round booty. But there is one topic that is off limits and not open for discussion, and that is sex with his wife or woman. The majority of the men I know will not discuss this with another man.

He might with another woman. But he will brag about all that good, freaky sex he is getting from his side chick, his jump-off, his freak on the side, his booty baby. Yes, ladies, all his buddies know about you and all the freaky things you can do.

3. The Horny Cheater: This cheater cheats for no other reason than he or she wants sex. It can be casual sex with someone he or she has just met or personal sex with someone he or she has known for a period of time. It can also be sex for money that he or she pays a person to do things with or to him or her that the person he or she is married to or in a relationship will not do. He or she may be ashamed or afraid to ask his or her partner to do or perform a sex act that he or she likes because he or she is afraid of what he or she might think about him or her. This person loves sex and will have it all the time with anyone. His or her only goal is to get his or her sexual desires met by any and all means.

The Married Women and the Women in Relationship Cheaters

*M*any times I have asked this question of the married women and the women in a relationship that I was having sex with: Why are you cheating? I always got a lot of different answers, but these five answers I got every time. Guys, this is why your wife or woman is cheating on you.

1. He doesn't appreciate me anymore. We never do anything together.
2. He doesn't show me any love or affection.
3. He no longer finds me attractive.
4. He says mean and hurtful things to me. He is abusive toward me.
5. This is the number one answer wives and women gave me for cheating: He has been cheating on me for months or years, and I'm damn tired of it.

Guys, these are the reason that wives and women gave me for cheating on you. I don't understand how you can be with a woman for ten, fifteen, twenty, or thirty-plus years and you still haven't learned how to treat your woman—how to appreciate her and the things she does for you, how to compliment her and say nice things to her, how to show her love and affection, and how to be honest, faithful, and loyal to her. Now not all men cheat on their wives or women. Not all women cheat on their husbands. This book is not for them. To the men and women who are cheating, and you know who you are, listen up. I am talking to you.

As a true player, I learned a lot over the years about marriage and relationships and how they can go from a woman loving her man with all her heart to a woman who can't stand to see the sight of him. Guys, I never met a bad woman, but I have been with women who have gone bad. The majority of the time, it is because of something a man has done to her. Guys, women are not cheaters by nature. They become cheaters after you cheat on her, break her heart, beat her, disrespect her, or lie to her. All the time you are doing this, you are thinking that angel you have at home would never do you wrong. Guys, let me share something with you and my experiences with those angels that I had back in the day. The angel you call your wife or woman cheats with me not because she likes me but because she no longer loves you.

Women Are Creative Cheaters

*G*uys, women are very creative cheaters. Women put thought into what they are doing, unlike a man. Here is my list of women cheaters from back in the day that I cheated with and what they told their men. I broke them down into four categories.

A. The going to the laundromat cheater
B. The going to the grocery store cheater
C. The going and get my nails and toes done cheater
D. The going to pay the bills cheater

A. The laundromat cheater: Guys, this woman will have you load up the car with four or five bundles of clothes so she can go wash them after she gets off work. She knows that you know it will take her about two hours to do them. When she walks in the house at 6:30 or 7:00, you are cool and don't have anything to say because you now have clean boxers, socks, shirts, and pants to wear. Guys, actually she took a little longer for lunch and did the laundry on her lunch hour, and now she has two hours to give me all that good, freaky sex. When she gets home, you don't notice that smile or glow on her face. All you want her to do is get rid of the kids so you can leave and go play video games, smoke weed, and drink with your boys.

B. The grocery store cheater: Guys, this woman tells you she is going to the grocery store to buy groceries after she gets off work. Actually, your woman has given the grocery list and the money to a girlfriend and she has purchased the groceries, and they are at her house. After she gets off work, she stops by my place, and we have good, freaky sex. She picks the groceries up on the way home, and you never notice that she was gone for a few of hours but only has two bags of groceries to last a whole month because when she brings the food into the house, you are ready for her to cook you something to eat so you can watch the game.

C. The nail, toes, and hair cheater: Guys, this woman doesn't have to come up with any creative way to cheat on you. All she has to do is tell you after work she is going to the salon. She knows it is a Friday night. She can come home looking just like she did when she went to work and you will never notice. She doesn't care if I messed that hair up during sex. She knows you will never notice her because you can't wait for her to get home so you can leave and go to the club or go be with your other women.

D. The I am going to pay the bills cheater: Guys, this woman knows she gets a pass once a month to cheat. She knows once a month all she has to do is tell you she is going to pay the bills and she can come home a little later than usual. She knows she can stay out as long as she likes because she is paying all or the majority of the bills. She knows you are not concerned what time she comes home as long as you have lights, internet, and cable. You don't know she pays the bills online at work. When she gets off, she comes by my house and gives me all that good, freaky sex. You don't notice her or what time she gets home because you are playing video games, smoking, drinking, and texting on your phone or on Facebook.

Guys, there you have it—the four cheaters and how they did it back in the day. They might be doing things different now. Guys, ask yourself these questions.

1. Why does my wife or woman go wash clothes at the laundromat when we have a washer and dryer in our apartment?
2. Why does my wife or woman tell me she bought groceries for the whole month but we always run out of food in a couple of weeks?
3. Why does my wife or woman's hair and nails look the same way as they did when she left for work after coming from getting them done? What do they look like when she comes home?
4. Why does my wife or woman shop online but goes out to pay her bills?

My Woman Is Not Cheating; She Has the Kids

$\mathcal{G}$uys, I can't tell you how many times I have heard you say this just because your woman or wife left home with the kids. Let me share this with you. Just because your wife or woman left home with the kids doesn't mean she is with the kids. Guys, as a true player back in the day, I learned if a woman has been mistreated by her husband or man and she makes up her mind to cheat, there is nothing that is going to stop her. Guys, if you wife or woman's family or girlfriends don't like you for the way you treat her, they will help her cheat on you, just like your family and friends help you cheat on her. Here are three ways married women and women in a relationship found ways to cheat.

1. The pizza party or child birthday party cheater
2. The kids and I are going to my girlfriend's house cheater
3. The kids and I are going to the movies cheater

Guys, how many times has your wife or woman said one of these things to you and you got happy because she and the kids are out of the house? Now you can get on Facebook and talk to other women or take naked selfies and send them to her or leave and go to your woman's house. Guys, the majority of the wives and women are doing just what they say they are. I am talking about the few who have gotten tired of you cheating on her, dogging her out, beating her, and disrespecting her. She has had enough, and now she just doesn't care anymore.

1. The pizza party are child birthday party cheater: Guys, your wife or woman uses these two events to cheat because she knows by telling you she is taking the kids to one of them, you know she will be away from the house all day Saturday and you can go get a haircut and spend the rest of the day with your other woman because she is with the kids and won't be blowing your phone up. Actually, your kids are in the bounce house or the ball box or playing video games, and they don't care where Mom is. Your woman has left and is now with me or another man giving us all

that freaky sex and doing all those freaky things to us just like your other woman is doing to you. If the kids ask, "Where is my mom?" her girlfriend tells them she will be back and she went to the store for ice cream. Guys, you are too dumb to notice that every Saturday your wife or woman and the kid have a party to go to because you see this as a way to spend the whole day with your other woman, you dumb ass.

2. The kids and I are going to my girlfriend's house cheater: Guys, this cheater actually truly amazed me, a true player, with her level of creative cheating. Your wife or woman tells you she and the kids are going over to her girlfriend's house, and they do. You see this as an opportunity to spend some time with your other woman. When she gets there, she meets one or two more girlfriends. They drink, eat, and have a good time. Then your woman gets a text that says, "I'm outside." Your woman gets up and leaves with me or the guy outside. Now she is not worried about the kids. They are in the back room playing video games and having a good time. If one does come out and asks, "Where is my mom?" her girlfriend just says she went to get pizza and will be back soon. Now you are out getting all that freaky sex from your other woman, and your wife or woman is out giving me or another man all that good, freaky sex. You are thinking what a good time you are having and she is having a boring night with her girlfriend, you dumb ass.

3. The kids and I are going to the movies cheater: Guys, your wife or woman sees this as an opportunity to get a quickie. She knows she doesn't have a lot of time. She meets her girlfriend and her kids at the movies, and they buy tickets for two different movies—the kids' movies and tickets for themselves to see a separate movie. She makes sure they the kids have candy, soda, and popcorn. She knows the average child's movie lasts an hour maybe an hour and a half and she doesn't have a lot of time to get her freak on. She tells the kids that she and her girlfriend will be down the hall watching another movie. Then she leaves, not going to watch a movie but to meet me or her other guy for some good quickie sex. If by chance one of the kids comes and asks for their mom, the girlfriend just

tells them she went to the car to get something and she will be back in a minute and for the kid go back and watch his or her movie.

Guys, there you have it. These are some of the ways that your wife or woman used to cheat back in the day. They are probably better at it now than they were back in the day. Ask yourself how many times have you heard your wife or woman say she and the kids were going to these places. Guys, I leave you with this question: Who's making love to your old lady while you are out making love?

Guys, Women Are Selective Cheaters

Guys, women are not random cheaters like men. When they do decide to cheat, they are very selective about the man they cheat with. They will not go out and find a man at the club, a bar, in the park, or walking down the street to cheat with. No, when a woman decides to cheat, the majority of the time it's with a man in her inner circle. Women rarely cheat outside that circle. She knows him and always wondered what it would be like to sleep with him. This could be the guy at work who always compliments her on her looks or dress, that guy at church who always has a word of comfort and something encouraging to say to her, your homeboy, or a family member who is always telling her how beautiful she is and how she can do better and if she were with him, he would treat her like a queen. Women cheat with men they feel comfortable with. I can't tell you how many times a married woman has told me that. That's why I was so successful. I made a women feel comfortable. Guys, women are very sensitive, emotional, and compassionate creatures, and they need to know and feel that their husband or man cares about them. The things you say and do have a lot to do with how your woman feels and acts. If your woman is not happy then your home is not a happy home, and then you step out to find happiness in the arms of another woman. For months or years your wife or woman put up with all your mess, and one day she decided that two can play that game. This is not all women but some, and your woman might be that one. Guys, like I said, out of all the married women I have had sex with, I never had sex with a bad woman. The married women I had sex with were all good women gone bad, and it was all because of something her husband or man did or was not doing to her.

Who Is More Observant When
It Comes to Cheating?

*Y*es, guys, from my personal experience, women are more observant than men when it comes to cheating. Guys, the majority of women can tell when you are cheating because they notice things about you and you don't even have a clue. When a man begins to cheat on his woman, his woman notices a change. You change your habits, routine, and dress. She notices how you act and talk and the things you do. She notices all these things about you. They tell her you are cheating or your dumb ass is up to something. Guys, we never notice anything about our wives or women because we think we have our stuff together at home and our loving wives or women will never cheat on us, even though we have caused her heartache and pain, she has busted us with other women, we have made children outside our marriage, and we gave her a STD and blamed her. We as men do all of these things to our good women, and we think to ourselves, *My woman has no reason to cheat on me.* Guys, let me ask you this. Just how much do you know about your wife or woman? Do you notice her and the things she does? Let's see, guys. How much do you know about your wife or woman? Can you answer any of these question about the woman you say you love?

1. What is your wife or woman's favorite color, and her favorite food?
2. When is her birthday? When is your anniversary?
3. What color dress did your wife wear to work? What color pants did she have on when she left the house? What color blouse did she have on?

Guys, your wife or woman probably got dressed in front of you and you didn't even notice what she wearing to work. But I bet your boys notice. I bet the guy at work notices. I bet the guy who attends her church notices. Guys, you have just made the decision easy for your wife or woman to cheat on you because you are not paying any attention to her and those guys are. Your wife or woman needs to know she has your attention. She needs to hear your compliments. She needs to know that you still find her attractive and sexy. She needs to know you care for her. She needs you to tell her how much you love her. Guys, she needs these things and more from you. They might sound small, unmeaningful, and insignificant to you, but to her coming from you these things mean a lot.

Guys, There Are Three Reasons Why Women Cheat

Guys, in my personal experience with having sex with hundreds of women, I have concluded that women cheat for three reasons. Now I'm not saying these are the three only reasons your wife or woman cheats on you I'm sure you have given her a lot and she has a lot of reasons to choose from. These are in my personal opinion the three reasons that over the years women have told me why they cheat.

1. Anger
2. Revenge
3. A broken heart

1. Anger: This is a way for your wife or woman to get back at you, her husband or man, after she has caught you cheating with another woman—a friend or a family member or maybe with someone she knows. Guys, when your wife or woman cheats on you out of revenge, this is payback. This is her last resort. This mean she has tried to work things out with you. You have told her over and over and time and time again you are done cheating and it will never happen again, and you keep doing it. Your wife begs you to stop cheating. She has pleaded with you to stop cheating. You just keep cheating till she is fed up with all your lies and broken promises. She feels like this is the only way to get her point across to you. You have caused her hurt and pain for the last time, and now it's time for her to show you how it feels to have your heart broken. Guys, you have just made a good woman go bad. You have just made cheating on you her final option.

2. Revenge: Guys, when your wife or woman cheats on you out of revenge, this usually means that the marriage or relationship is over, and you have messed up so bad that nothing you can do or say will fix the problem. She is filled up with pain and hurt, and she wants you to experience the same pain and hurt that she is feeling. That's why she

chooses a man close to you to cheat with—your brother, best friend, dad, uncle, or cousin. She feels this is the only way she has to let you feel the hurt and pain she is feeling. Normally she would not give these guys a second thought. But revenge has taken over, and she just wants you to feel the hurt and pain she is feeling.

3. The broken heart: Guys, the majority of the married women I have had sex with came to me with a broken heart. A woman's heart is very delicate and fragile thing. You must handle it with care and love. Guys, when your wife or woman cheats on you after you have broken her heart, she is not doing it out of revenge or anger. She is doing it out of sorrow, confusion, and disappointment. The majority of the time it's not even about the sex. She just wants a man to love the hurt away. She just wants to feel that she is loved and needed.

Guys, there you have it. This is why women cheat. These are not all the reasons why women cheat. Your wife or woman has her own. Guys, remember that the majority of women are not cheaters. It is not in their nature. She became a cheater most of time because of something you, her husband or her man, is doing or is not doing. Guys, the next time you are with that other woman, ask her why she is cheating on her man. I bet she gives you the same answer your wife or woman is giving to the man she is cheating with.

How Do I Know If My Wife
Is Cheating on Me?

*G*uys, I can't answer that, but I can give you five things to look out for.

1. When she stops asking where you are going.
2. When she stops worrying about where you are.
3. When she stops caring about what time you come home.
4. When she stops wondering if you are coming home.
5. When she stops calling around looking for you.

Guys, these are just five things you can look for I'm sure there are many more that might help you to know if you wife or woman may be cheating are getting ready to cheat. Guys if your wife or woman has stop doing these things please stop doing the things you are doing before it's too late before you drive her into the arms of another man. Guys remember a good woman in your life will make for a happy life. A good woman gone bad can make your life a living *hell*.

Ladies, There Are Three Types of Male Cheaters

adies there are three types of male cheater. I know you know that there are many more. But these are three most common cheaters ladies have told me about, so let's see if you are living with one of these cheaters.

1. Dumb cheater
2. It's not my fault cheater
3. It's your fault I'm cheating cheater

1. Dumb cheater: You catch this guy cheating time and time again. He is too damn dumb to change. You know better than he does what he will do before he does it. There is no challenge for you to try to catch him cheating. His dumb ass makes the same mistake over and over. He makes it too easy for you. But you stay with him for your family or you just love his dumb ass. You hope he will stop cheating or at least stop making it so easy for you to catch his dumb ass.

2. It's not my fault cheater: When you bust this guy cheating, it is never his fault he is cheating on you. When you bust him with condoms in his car or pocket, they are never his. He was holding them for his brother or homeboy. When you bust him with naked women photos in his phone, he says, "I don't know her. It's not my fault she's sending me her picture." When you find panties or bras or weave hair in his car or apartment, he tells you he let his brother or homeboy use his car or apartment. He says, "They belong to his woman. It's not my fault she left them there." Ladies, every time you bust his ass cheating, it is never his fault.

3. It's your fault I'm cheating cheater: Ladies, you tell me this is the worst cheater of all. This cheater when you bust him, it's never his fault. It is always yours. He tells you he is cheating on you because you have gained weight, you have let yourself go and you don't look the same, you don't

cook or clean house like you used to, you don't have any time for him, or you are too busy at work all the time. It's your fault he cheats because you stopped giving him sex. There you have it, ladies. Your husband or man is cheating on you, and it's all your fault. I know you have lots more reasons for why your husband or man is cheating on you, but the number one reason he cheats is because he is tired of being in the marriage or relationship and he wants out. He doesn't want to be with you anymore, and he is not man enough to tell you.

Cheating Men—Why Do They Cheat?

*L*adies, we as men need no reason to cheat on our wives or women. If we see a woman we want to have sex with, there is nothing you can do or say to stop us. It doesn't matter how you, our wives or women, look, how freaky you are in the bedroom, how good you can cook and clean house, or how much money you have. You can be as beautiful as Halle Berry and Beyoncé, and we as men will cheat on you. You can have a body like Nicki Minaj and we will still cheat on you. You can have millions like Oprah Winfrey and we will still cheat on you. You can cook in the kitchen like Rachael Ray and we will still cheat. You can perform any freaky sex act we can imagine and we will still cheat on you. Ladies, you can have all the freaky threesomes for him and he will still cheat on you. You can slide down a pole with hundred-dollar bill shooting out of your ass and he will still cheat on you and continue to blame you for it. Ladies, not all men are cheaters, but the ones who are cheating do it because they want to. It has nothing to do with you. Men will cheat and blame you, his wife or woman, for it just to justify his cheating and make you like feel it's all your fault. Ladies, your man needs no good reason to cheat on you other than he has seen a new piece of ass and he just has to try it out. Your man doesn't need a reason to cheat on you, but he does need someone to blame his cheating on, and that someone is you.

Cheating—Who's Better at It, Men or Women?

*W*ell let's find out. Here's a list of ten question you can ask yourself about your husband or man or your wife or woman. Let's see how you do. Cheaters, answer these ten questions.

1. How many times have you caught you husband or man cheating?
2. How many times have you caught your wife or woman cheating?
3. Can you tell when your husband or man is cheating on you?
4. Can you tell when your wife or woman is cheating on you?
5. Wife or woman, do you think you can find evidence of your husband or man cheating today?
6. Husband or man, do you think you can find evidence of your wife or woman cheating today?
7. Women, on a scale from one to ten, how skilled do you think your husband or man is at cheating and getting away with cheating (1–3, Excellent, 4–6, Good, 7–9, He might think he is getting away with it, but I know his ass is cheating, 10, His dumb ass needs to stop cheating because I am tired of catching his dumb ass)?
8. Men, on a scale from one to ten, how skilled do you think your wife or woman is at cheating and getting away with it (1–3, Excellent, 4–6, Good, 7–9, She is doing something, I just don't know what it is, 10, My wife or woman is not smart enough to cheat on me and get away with it)?
9. Men, when you are having sex with the woman you are cheating with, where do you do it? A. At her place B. Motel or hotel C. The car or the park D. At the home that you and your wife or woman share.
10. Women, when you are having sex with the man you are cheating with, where do you it? A. At his place B. Motel or hotel C. The car or park D. The home that you and your husband or man share.

Cheaters, how did you do? Who do you think are better cheaters, men or women? Now tell me who the better cheater is in your home—the husband or the wife?

Dumb and Dumber Cheater

These are some stories of some of my male friends and how they got busted cheating. Like I said, women are creative and selective cheaters. Men just don't care. We don't think or give a damn. We will cheat with anybody, anytime, anywhere and this is the story of those cheaters.

My New Truck Got Me Busted

This guy, let's call him George, was a good friend. His wife bought him a new pickup truck for his forty-fifth birthday. It was very a nice and was fully loaded. It had all the newest technology. It had something that was very new at the time called On Star GPS. With this device if you ever locked yourself out of your car, you could call On Star and tell them, and they could send a signal to your car and unlock the door. How cool is that? The truck had something else that was new called GPS. With this you could get turn-by-turn directions to anywhere you wanted to go. You would never get lost again. How cool is that?

Where the Hell Is My Truck!

George's truck was very nice. It was a chick magnet. He got a lot of women with that truck. One night we were at the club, and George met this young lady and knew he had to have her. She was fine, with a pretty face, small waist, big breasts, and round booty George knew she would be his that night, and she was. At about 1:00 a.m. I left the club and went home and went to sleep. About 4:00 a.m., I got a call from George. He was at the motel. He said he was leaving, and when he walked outside his room, his truck was gone. He said he needed me to come get him and take that lady home. I asked him, "Where are you?" He said he was at the motel. I got up and picked him and the woman up. We drove around but didn't find the truck. I ask him, "What are you going to do? What are you going to tell your wife?" After driving around for an hour. he came up with the lie that someone stole the truck from the gambling shack while he was playing poker. I thought he could do better, but a lie is a lie.

Smart Wife, Dumb Cheater

Well about six o'clock that morning, he called his wife telling her someone had stolen the truck and I was bringing him home. He told her when he got home he was going to call the police and report it stolen. He felt better about the lie, but he was still hurt about the loss of his new truck. I took him home, and when we pulled up in his driveway, the garage door went up and there was his truck. We couldn't believe it. Just then George's wife came walking out of the garage with three trash bags filled with his clothes. She threw them down at his feet. She told him she was the one who got the truck from the motel. He was shocked, and so was I. How did she find the motel? How did she get the truck home? George put his clothes in the trunk of my car, and I drove him to his mother's house. I didn't hear from George for a few weeks. One day I got a call from him. He was back with his wife and she had forgiven him. I was glad to hear that. I asked him how she got the truck from the motel to his garage. This is what he told me. His wife woke up about two o'clock that morning and he was not in bed, so she called the On Star people and told them her son had snuck out the house and she thought he was out joyriding in the truck. She asked if they could send her GPS directions to the truck so she could find him. They did send the turn-by-turn direction to where the truck was. She got up and went and got a girlfriend. They came to the motel, and she drove the truck home. This dumb cheater got busted by the technology in his new truck.

Cheater Number Two—Viagra Got Me Busted

Story number two is about my friend Roy. Roy was a good friend of mine. He was in his early fifties, and there were two things Roy loved doing—drinking Crown Royal and having sex with young women, and he did a lot of both. But Roy needed a little help in the sex area, so we would buy Viagra pills from the other old guys who would be at the gambling shack where we all went. Roy's doctor would not prescribe him Viagra because he had high blood pressure and a bad heart. But this didn't stop Roy from doing what he loved—drinking and having sex with young women.

Viagra, Alcohol, and Young Women Don't Mix

One night I was at the gambling shack. All the young women in the neighborhood would come there. They knew this was the place to be on weekends because all the old men with big money would be there. Roy would get one and give her anything she wanted. After a couple of hours, Roy and a young woman left. He said he would be back in a couple of hours. I didn't see Roy for about a month after that night. I called him a few times to see if he was okay. He didn't say much on the phone. He just said, "We will talk later." I asked him where had he been and what he had been doing. All the young women were asking me about him. What he told me then blew me away. He said that night he and that woman left and went to the motel, he almost died. He said he had been drinking all day, and before he left he took a blue pill. When he made it to the motel, he and that young woman smoked a joint. He said he was ready then. Then he started to feel hot, and his chest started to hurt. His eyes turned red, and he started to sweat. He started to shake and tremble. Just then the young woman, who was already in the bed waiting on him, asked, "When are you coming to bed?" He said he tried to answer but couldn't because his face had become disfigured.

Damn! How Can I Explain This to My Wife?

Well after a few minutes, the young woman got tired of waiting on him to come out of the restroom. She got out the bed and came in to see what was taking him so long. He said when she opened the restroom door, she saw him sitting on the toilet shaking and trembling. She ran and told the motel manager to call 911. This man need an ambulance. They called the ambulance, and it took him to the emergency room at the hospital. As they were working on him in the emergency room, the nurse asked him if there was anyone he wanted them to contact. He said, "Yes, my wife," so they called his wife. After they were done working on him, the doctor told him he had a mild heart attack and he would be fine. After they were done with him, he could go home. The doctor asked him what he was doing at the time he had the heart attract. He said he didn't want to tell the doctor he was at the motel with a woman, so he said he was at a friend's house playing cards. He said the doctor looked at him funny and told him that the ambulance driver said he picked him up from the motel. He said he came clean and told the whole story to the doctor. The doctor told him to lay there and rest and he would be back to check on him. His wife was on her way. He was still out of it from the medication the doctor had given him, and he noticed how the nurses kept coming into his room and laughing. Then he said he felt his penis burning and he remembered he had taken that Viagra pill. He said he looked down and his penis was standing up under that little gown like a tent. Just then the doctor and his wife walked in, and he saw the look of shock on her face as she pointed at it and said, "What's that? I haven't seen that in months." He said he didn't know how to explain this to his wife, and to make it worse, the doctor kept him overnight and his wife chewed him out all night.

Cheater Number Three

I lost my wife and my business and got a new baby by cheating.

This is the story about a friend, let's call him Richard, who was a successful businessman. He owned his own restaurant. Now Richard was in his late fifties and a nice-looking guy who loved young women. He would tell me about how he was having sex with the waitresses who worked for him. I often told him, "Man, you need to stop that because your wife comes in all the time to do the books, and you are going to get busted one day." He would tell me how everything was cool. The women wouldn't tell on him because he treated them right and gave them extra money when they needed it. One day I stopped by the restaurant for dinner on my way home from work and Richard and I were talking. He was telling me about the new waitress he had just hired and how fine she was and how he was getting all that good, freaky sex from her and the other waitress was jealous of her. I told him, "Man, that's not cool. You should never get your honey from the same place you make your money." He laughed at me and said, "Man, I know what I am doing. I got this under control."

Cheating Cost Me Everything

Well a couple months went by, and I didn't see Richard. I traveled a lot on my job and wasn't able to get by the restaurant. One day I was on my way home, and I stopped by the restaurant to see my boy. When I drove into the parking lot, the building was closed, and the windows were all boarded up. I got out of my car and walked around to the front of the business. There was a sign on the door that said, "Out of Business." I thought to myself, *How could this restaurant go out of business? It was always busy, and the people loved the food.* I tried calling Richard on the phone, but his phone had been turned off. I didn't see or hear from Richard for a few months until one night I was at the club and he walked up to me. I didn't know who he was at first. Like I said, Richard was a nice-looking guy in his late fifties, but this guy looked like he was in his seventies. I asked, "Man, what happened to you, and why did you close down the restaurant?"

What the Hell! You Mean You Are Pregnant?

Richard told me, "Man, buy me a drink and I will tell you the whole story." We went to the bar. Richard started drinking and talking, and I couldn't believe what came out of his mouth. He said after he dated that young woman for a few months, she stopped wanting to be his woman and started wanting to be his wife. Then she told him he had to leave his wife and move in with her. Then she dropped a bomb on him. She told him she was three months pregnant and Richard was the father.

I asked him, "Man, how old was that woman?"

He said, "Twenty-seven, the same age as my youngest daughter."

I said, "Damn! Man, I knew you like them young, but damn!"

That was all I could say. He said he told her to get abortion and he would pay for it. She said she was not getting an abortion and for Richard to take that money and get a divorce. He said to her he was not leaving his wife. She told him she was telling his wife, and she did. He said his wife went crazy. She put him out of the house, took the money out of their bank account, and divorced him. He had to sell the restaurant to pay the lawyers and his wife.

He said, "Man, she got everything—the house, the car, and the money." He said he had to move back home with his mother.

I asked, "What happened to your young woman?"

He said, "When the money was gone, she was gone."

After telling me his story, Richard asked, "Man, can you buy me another drink?"

I reached into my pocket, pulled out a twenty-dollar bill, and said, "Man, buy yourself a bottle." Richard got up and left, but there is a happy ending to this story. Richard is now the proud father of a cute baby girl that he is paying child support for.

Ladies, There Are Some Dumb Female Cheaters out There

Ladies, I haven't forgotten about you. There are some dumb female cheaters out there too. This is the story about three of my female friends. They lost out on a good man by cheating. This story is called, "I accept you as a package and leave as a package."

Joyce is friend number one. Joyce was a young lady in her late thirties with four kids by four different baby daddies who were either in jail or MIA. She was still an attractive lady with a nice shape and could get just about any man she wanted. She was a hardworking lady who took good care of her kids. But she was always attracted to the wrong guys—the players, the ballers, the guys who had the nice cars and had lots of money to spend on her. One day we were talking, and she was telling me about this guy who had been trying to get with her for a while. She met him at the grocery store. She said they had talked and before she left, they exchanged numbers. She said he seemed like a nice guy, but he wasn't her type. But he had been calling her and asking her to go out on a date, and she kept putting him off. I told her to give him a try since nothing else was working for her, so she did. She told me he was a really nice guy and very respectable. He was a gentleman and knew how to treat a lady.

I asked her, "Are you going to continue to see this guy?"

She said yes, and they began to date. I met him. He was a nice guy, and I could tell he was crazy about Joyce. I was happy for both of them. She told me that she really liked this guy. He was just what she was looking for. He was good to her and her kids, and they liked him. He had a good-paying job and his own place. She said she told him that she was a package deal with her kids. He said he was all right with that. They dated a few months. Then he asked her and the kids to move in with him. She did, and things were good for about a year. Then she got a text from baby daddy number two. He was getting out of prison and wanted to see her and his baby. She asked me what she should do.

I said, "Talk it over with your man, and then you two decide on what you should do."

She did. They both decided that she would meet him at her mother's house so he could see his child. But I could see in her eyes she was just as excited to see him again as he was to see her. Everything went well. The baby daddy began to spend time with the baby. Then he started to spend time with Joyce and the baby. Then he started to spend a lot of time with Joyce without the baby. Yes, they were having a sexual relationship. This went on for a few months until Joyce's man found out about it and demanded that she and her kids get the hell out of his house.

She said she asked him, "What about the kids? They love you."

He said, "I love them too, but you should have thought about that before you cheated on me. I accepted you as a package deal, and now I am putting your ass out as a package deal."

Poor Joyce had to move out and move back home with her mother, and baby daddy went back to the penitentiary for violating his parole.

I Had It All and Lost It All

Deborah is friend number two. This story is about my friend named Deborah. She had it all. Every woman dreams about the big house, the nice cars, gold and platinum credit cards, and a man who loves her very much and works hard and provides her with everything she wants—except a child.

Deborah's husband was eighteen years older than she was and already had grown kids and didn't want any more. Deborah didn't have any kids and always wanted children. They were both good friends of mine, and I could understand both points of view. Deborah's husband was a manager for a large corporation, and he traveled a lot. Sometimes he would be gone for days at a time. I guess when you've married a woman who is much younger, you should give her more than cars and credit cards to keep her happy. He was out of town on business a lot, and Deborah started saying she was being neglected in the bedroom when he came home, and he was not giving her what she needed sexually. Even though she said she loved him, she had to get her something on the side, and she did.

For months she had an affair, and her husband never knew until one day a friend of theirs saw Deborah and her new man out at dinner. When they left the restaurant and went to the car, the man she was with got in on the driver side and was driving his car. Well that news got around first and made it to her husband. He was upset and left her, but he forgave her and they got back together.

A couple months later, the happy couple had a party and told all of their friends they were pregnant. Deborah was very happy, but her husband didn't look that excited by the news. A few months went by, and the couple continued to have problems. After the baby was born, they decided to get a divorce and go their separate ways. During the divorce proceedings, Deborah's husband's lawyer presented a document stating he was not the father of the child. He had a procedure done years ago and was not able to have kids, and the child Deborah had was not his. The judge ordered a DNA test, and it revealed the child she had was not his. Things didn't go too well for Deborah. After that day, she went from having a big house to living in government-assisted housing. She went from driving a nice car to riding the bus, and she went from having gold and platinum credit cards to only having a government-issued EBT card. She lost everything, all because she wanted to cheat.

Story Number Three—form Saint to Sinner

Wanda is friend number three. This is a story about a longtime friend of mine named Wanda. Wanda and I have been friends since grade school. Wanda comes from a family with a strong Christian background and strong family morals and values. She was a preacher's daughter, and all the kids made fun of her because she was a little overweight and didn't dress whorish like the other girls in the neighborhood. But she was my friend, and she hooked me up with the girls at her church. Wanda's dad did not allow her to hang out with boys, but he knew my mom and he was okay with me. We were friends long after school. Then she went off to college. After that I didn't see her for a few years. Then one night I was at the club and I saw a fine lady on the dance floor. She was sexy, and I walked up to her and looked and said, "Wanda?"

She said, "Yes, Randy, it's me."

I couldn't believe what I was seeing. That little fat girl was now a grown, fine-ass woman. We had a few drinks and caught up on times. She said she had been dating a guy in her father's church and that she was going to get married in a few months. I gave her a big hug and told her congratulations and I was happy for her. She told me who the guy was. I knew him. He was a good guy.

Just then a guy walked up to her, put his arm around her waist, and said, "Baby, are you ready to go?"

She looked at him and told him, "Yes, baby, I am."

Now I knew the guy she was engaged to, and this guy was not him. She gave me a hug and said, "We will talk later."

A few weeks later I ran into Wanda at a friend's house party. I asked her, "Who was that guy you were with at the club?"

She said, "He was just a friend I knew from back in the day. We met at the club for drinks. There is nothing going on between us."

One Picture Is Worth a Thousand Words

Well, it was the day of the wedding. I was getting dressed, and then I got a text from Wanda. I read it, and the text said, "My wedding photo." I looked at the picture and asked myself, "Why is Wanda sending me a picture of herself naked bent over with her ass up in the air." Just then another picture came. I looked at it and asked myself again, "Why is Wanda sending me a picture and she is naked on her back with her legs up in the air spread from east to west?" Then another picture came, and I asked myself, "Why is Wanda sending me a picture of herself on her knees with her head between a man's legs?"

Then I started to get texts from people asking me if I saw the pictures of Wanda and saying she had called off the wedding. Well since I was already dressed, I went down to the church to find out what was going on. When I pulled up, a fire department ambulance was pulling off, and there were some people gathered in the parking lot of the church, all looking at their cell phones. I walked up to the crowd, and someone said the pastor had a heart attack after he received those pictures of his daughter.

Well, it turned out the whole church congregation, family, friends, and coworkers had received those pictures, as well as the groom and his family. By the way, the groom was in the church crying like a baby. I found out later from a close friend of Wanda's that she had stopped seeing the guy she was cheating with, and he didn't take it well. Somehow he got her phone and downloaded all her contact information and sent those special pictures that she had taken with him to everybody. It was all because she ended the cheating relationship she was having with him. Well one good thing did come out of this. I finally got a chance to see Wanda naked—nice.

There you have my stories about my friends and how cheating changed their lives. I believe people who cheat thinks they have a good reason for cheating on the person they say they love. The majority of the people think their reason justifies their action. I don't understand how could you hurt and bring pain to the person you vow to spend the rest of your life with, till death do you part—the person you vow to love and cherish forever. I believe everybody enters a marriage with the thought of being with that person the rest of his or her life. You want to live a long, happy, rich, and fulfilling life with that person, but somewhere something happened. Things start to change. You somehow find your distance from that person. You are no longer attracted to that person. You are no longer in love with that person. But you stay. You have your own reasons. It may be financial, comfort, convenience, or the child or children. You will spend years with this person and all along you want out, but you just don't want to start over. So you start cheating or accept the fact that the other person is cheating, and you live with it. Marriage is a commitment that two people make to each other that should last a lifetime. Unfortunately, many times it doesn't. Every marriage will end at some point and not all the time in the way we think. Please don't allow yours to end because you brought hurt, pain, and suffering into the person's life who you vowed you would love forever. Remember, not all marriages will last forever. Not all marriages are meant to be, but all marriages must have love, trust, and God in them to work.

So cheaters, ask yourself these ten things about your marriage and why are you cheating.

1. Is my marriage worth saving?
2. Am I willing to lose everything we have worked so hard to build?
3. Will cheating with another person make my life better?
4. Would I want my husband or wife to cheat on me?
5. Is the person I am cheating with better than the person I am married to?

6. Other than good, freaky sex, what do the person I'm cheating with and I have in common?
7. If I put as much time in trying to make my marriage work as I put in cheating, could I save my marriage?
8. What do I have to gain from cheating? Will it solve all my problems and make my life better?
9. Is cheating my only option to fix my marriage?
10. I know if I get caught cheating, it will hurt my husband or wife, so why do I continue to do it?

That's it, cheater. Your reason for cheating is yours and yours alone, and why you do it only you know. Who do you think does it better, men or women? Do you really want to know? But remember this—at one time you were very much in love with the person you are now cheating on. You are taking a chance of bringing pain, hurt, and heartache into his or her life. Does he or she deserve that? Please stop and think about these things you stand to lose if you are caught cheating.

1. The love and respect of your husband or wife
2. Your family
3. The respect from your family and friends
4. The joy that come from having a good husband or wife
5. Your job or your business.
6. Your right to see and visit your child or children
7. Your right to live in your own home
8. Your self-respect
9. Your life
10. All the things you both worked so hard to accomplish—your home, your car your property, and your money

Cheaters, please ask yourself, are you willing to lose all the things you love and cherish for a few moments of good, freaky sex?

A True Player

I am a retired true player with thirty-five years of true player experiences. That comes from having sex with hundreds of women, some married but mostly single, and yes, I used protection. I bet you ask what's the difference between a player and a true player. A true player don't lie, deceive, or manipulate women into having a relationship with him. He is always up front and honest with a woman about the kind of relationship he wants to have with her. A true player lets the woman decide if she wants to be with him. A true player let the woman know up front she is not the only woman he is seeing. A true player knows that not every woman is going to accept the kind of relationship he is looking to have with her, but he lets the woman make that choice, unlike the other guy.

A Little Advice

irst I would like to say I am not a marriage counselor, relationship expert, or life coach. What I am is a man who has been in all kinds of relationships, some good and some bad. I have heard every reason and excuse for why men and women chat, and none of them justifies hurting or breaking the heart of someone you say you love. None of them justifies breaking the vow you made before God to love this person for better or worse, though good times and bad times, till death do you part. Not all marriages will last forever, not all marriages are meant be, and not all people married for the right reason, but cheating is not the way a marriage should end. A marriage shouldn't end just because a person gained weight, or their looks changed, or their desire for sex is not what it used to be, or you are having money problems or health issues. Don't those things fall under for better or worse? Every marriage has problems, but trying to find the solution to your problem in the arms of someone else is not the answer.

Cheating—Who's better at It, Men or Women?

This is my answer. Men created cheating,
but women perfected it.

Look for these books coming soon:

Black People: Do Black Lives Matter to Black People
Baby Mama Drama is Why
The Good Fathers Get No
Credit and Recognition

Printed in the United States
By Bookmasters